Preface

For above forty years I have been a diligent collector of history, tradition, legend, custom, or folklore, whether from familiar or unfamiliar sources, relating to the festival of the Holy Nativity. I have drawn freely on such well-known stores of out-of-the-way knowledge as Brand's *Popular Antiquities* with the additions of Ellis, Hone's *Every Day Book*, *Table Book*, and *Ancient Mysteries*, *The Popish Kingdom* of Naogeorgus (Kirchmeyer) as translated by Barnaby Googe, Chambers's *Book of Days*, Husk's *Songs of the Nativity*, Miles's *Christmas in Ritual and Tradition*, and *The Home of a Naturalist* by Edmundson and Saxby; also from various publications of the Percy, Shakspere, and Surtees Societies. Moreover, I have gathered copiously from scarce pamphlets of the 17th and 18th centuries, from old chapbooks, newspaper paragraphs, and magazine articles old and new, and from contact with rustics in several counties. I must also acknowledge my indebtedness to Mr. Donald A. Mackenzie, for several valuable suggestions. The fruits of my gathering are briefly summarized in the following pages, in the hope that they may conduce to that " joy and pious mirth " wherewith we ought, all of us, to commemorate the best and greatest Gift of God to man.

T. G. CRIPPEN.

Contents

	Page
INTRODUCTION	1
ORIGIN OF CHRISTMAS	2
COINCIDENT FESTIVALS	9
NAMES OF CHRISTMAS	11
USE OF EVERGREENS	12
HOLLY AND IVY	14
LAUREL, ROSEMARY, FIR, ETC.	18
MISTLETOE	20
PLACING AND REMOVING EVERGREENS	25
CHRISTMAS GHOSTS	28
CHRISTMAS TALES	31
CHRISTMAS MUSIC—THE WAITS	35
OLD CHRISTMAS HYMNS	37
CHRISTMAS CAROLS	41
ORIGIN OF CAROLS	43
THE OLDEST ENGLISH CAROLS	49
LEGENDARY, MYSTICAL, AND MODERN CAROLS	54
USE OF CAROLS	61
CHURCH OBSERVANCES—ADVENT	65
CHURCH OBSERVANCES—CHRISTMAS BELLS	67
CHURCH OBSERVANCES—MIDNIGHT MASS	70
NATIVITY PLAYS	73
THE PRÆSEPIO	78
CRADLE-ROCKING: THE POSADA, ETC.	81
THE CHILDREN'S CHRISTMAS	84
PURITAN HOSTILITY TO CHRISTMAS	87
MUMMING	94

	Page
HODENING, SCHIMMEL, ETC.	97
WASSAILING	99
CHRISTMAS EVE	104
THE YULE LOG	108
CHRISTMAS CANDLES	114
THE CHRISTMAS FEAST	116
THE BOAR'S HEAD	126
CHRISTMAS SPORTS	130
MASKING	134
THE LORD OF MISRULE	135
YULE-FIRTH: "UNTHRIFTY FOLK"	142
CHRISTMAS GIFTS—SANTA CLAUS, ETC.	143
THE CHRISTMAS SHEAF	149
THE CHRISTMAS TREE	150
THE CHRISTMAS SHIP	155
CHRISTMAS BOXES	157
CHRISTMAS CARDS, ETC.	161
FAMILY REUNIONS—THE CHILDREN'S DAY	163
MISCELLANEOUS CHRISTMAS SUPERSTITIONS, ETC.	165
YULE-TIDE IN THULE	171
SUBSIDIARY FESTIVALS	175
NEW YEAR'S EVE—HAGMENA	182
OLD CHRISTMAS EVE: WASSAILING TREES	188
EPIPHANY	191
TWELFTH NIGHT	196
FEAST OF FOOLS, OR OF THE ASS	200
PLOUGH MONDAY, ETC.	203
CANDLEMAS	204
EPILOGUE	209
APPENDIX: ADDENDA AND CORRIGENDA	213
INDEX	215

CHRISTMAS
AND
CHRISTMAS LORE

BY

T. G. CRIPPEN

DETROIT • 1971
Gale Research Company • Book Tower

This is a facsimile reprint of the
1923 edition first published by
Blackie & Son Limited, London.

Library of Congress Catalog Card Number 69-16067

CHRISTMAS
AND CHRISTMAS LORE

17 257

LA MADONNA DEL GRANDUCA

From the painting by Raphael in the Palazzo Pitti, Florence.

A work of the master's Florentine period, formerly in the grand-ducal palace. Painted and modelled with extraordinary delicacy, the simple female beauty and tender modesty of the Madonna are but thinly concealed by the religious character of the picture.

List of Plates

Facing
Page

LA MADONNA DEL GRANDUCA · · · · *Frontispiece*
From the painting by Raphael

CUTTING THE MISTLETOE IN DRUIDICAL DAYS · · · 24
From the painting by Henri Motte

"GOD REST YE MERRY, GENTLEMEN" · · · · 64
From the painting by J. Seymour Lucas, R.A.

AFTER MIDNIGHT MASS, FIFTEENTH CENTURY · · · 72
From the painting by G. H. Boughton, R.A.

BRINGING IN THE YULE LOG, PENSHURST PLACE, KENT · 112
After Joseph Nash

CHRISTMAS REVELS: HADDON HALL, DERBYSHIRE · · · 136
After Joseph Nash

THE FIRST CHRISTMAS CARD (1846) · · · · · 160
After a design by J. C. Horsley, R.A.

THE WASSAILING OF THE APPLE TREES · · · · 184
From an old wood-cut

CHRISTMAS
AND CHRISTMAS LORE

1. INTRODUCTION

"Christmas!" Is there any other word in our whole English vocabulary that calls forth such a flood of joyous emotion as that which designates the Festival of Humanity—the day which we are accustomed to regard as "peculiarly the Home and Household Festival of England? Longed for as the season when our shining hearths, our domestic comforts, and our social felicity are the brightest under heaven; the chosen season of peace and goodwill, of family reunions, of happy visits, of friendly greetings, of interchange of gifts, of kindness to the poor, of mutual esteem and universal joy ": the blending of sport, mirth, and laughter with Faith, Hope, and Charity, this is a real English Christmas. Within, the house is gay with holly and ivy, laurel and fir; the mistletoe hangs in the place of honour, shimmering with pearls that seem to have dropped from Freyja's necklace Brising; the Yule log blazes on the hearth; the Christmas-tree towers aloft in faery splendour; and the Christmas candles burn in homely remembrance of the Star of Bethlehem. Without, the stars look as brightly down on an expanse of snow, deep and crisp and even, as once they looked upon those holy fields where shepherds watched their flocks by night. Borne upon the frosty air comes the merry chiming of Christmas bells, or mayhap the solemn tolling of the knell of the Prince of Darkness. And, mingling with the brazen music, we hear the sound of youthful voices caroling " Joy to the world ", or " Hark! the herald angels sing ", or, better still, that simplest and dearest of all our old English carols (case-hardened must be the heart that does not respond to it):

> " God rest you merry, gentlemen,
> Let nothing you dismay;
> Remember, Christ our Saviour
> Was born on Christmas day,
> To save us all from Satan's power,
> When we were gone astray:
> O tidings of comfort and joy!"

2. ORIGIN OF CHRISTMAS

Our topic is old Christmas customs and traditions; and the difficulty is, where to begin? Perhaps it is best to begin at the beginning and ask: " Where did Christmas come from?" Not from what secret recess did that hale and frosty giant emerge, with his jovial face and holly crown and steaming bowl, who smiles upon us from ten thousand pictures, and whom we instinctively recognize as " Father Christmas "; but how did the fashion arise of celebrating the birthday of our Lord on the 25th of December, not only

with religious observances but with feasting and
jollity? For there is no record, nor even any respectable tradition, of the actual date of our Saviour's birth.

Even the year is not absolutely certain. It is
generally agreed that the traditional date, A.U.C.
753 [1], is too late; for St. Matthew distinctly affirms
that " Jesus was born in Bethlehem of Judea in the
days of Herod the king ", and Herod died in A.U.C.
750. There must have been time, between the birth
of Jesus and the death of Herod, for the visit of the
wise men from the East, the retreat into Egypt, and
the Slaughter of the Innocents. The testimony of
St. Luke is by no means as decisive as at first glance
it seems to be. For one thing, the real meaning of
his remark about the census (ch. ii, 2) is very doubtful. Then it is uncertain whether " the fifteenth
year of Tiberius Cæsar " (ch. iii, 1) is counted from
A.U.C. 765, when he was associated with Augustus
in the Empire, or from the death of Augustus in
A.U.C. 767. Then the phrase " about 30 years old ",
in ch. iii, 23, may mean anything from 29 to 31; so
that Luke's indications of the year of the Nativity
are not more definite than " about A.U.C. 749 to
753 ". Nor does St. Matthew help us much by his
account of the Star, seen first in the East and then
over Bethlehem. There is indeed no necessity to
understand this as denoting either a new star or such
a conjunction of two or more stars as would make
them seem to coalesce; or a mere atmospheric meteor.
The most likely meaning of " His Star " is some such
celestial phenomenon as, interpreted by astrological

[1] *Anno Urbis Conditæ 753* = the 753rd year from the building of the city, i.e. Rome.

rules, would indicate the birth in Judea of someone destined to greatness. Now there was a remarkable conjunction of two planets in May, again in October, and yet again in November, A.U.C. 747, which astrologers would certainly think portended some great thing about to happen. We are nowhere told that Jesus was born exactly at the time when the " star " appeared; but it seems safe to conclude that His birth was at some time between the middle of A.U.C. 747 and the end of A.U.C. 749, i.e. 7 B.C. and 5 B.C.

This agrees with a very ancient tradition that, when our Lord was born, the temple (more correctly *gate*) of Janus at Rome was shut, in token of peace throughout the whole Roman dominion. Such an event had only occurred twice before the reign of Augustus; but it happened in A.U.C. 724, and again in A.U.C. 746, from which time the gate remained closed for several years.

> " No war, or battle's sound,
>> Was heard the world around;
> The idle spear and shield were high uphung;
>> The hookèd chariot stood
>> Unstained with hostile blood;
> The trumpet spake not to the armèd throng;
>> And kings sat still with awful eye,
> As if they surely knew their sovran Lord was by."

If the *year* of our Saviour's birth is thus open to question, the *day* is yet more uncertain. The days of His death and resurrection are clearly recorded in the Gospels, and, from the time of the Apostles until now, the anniversary of His resurrection victory has been almost universally observed. The birthday of the Church, too, the Day of Pentecost, was fixed by the Jewish Calendar, and from almost the earliest ages it has been kept as a joyful Christian anniversary. Very early, too, it became usual to consecrate the New Year to Him in whom all things become new, by a festival which was designed to commemorate at once His manifestation, His baptism, and His first miracle. But not until the third century do we find any attempt to fix with authority the day of His birth. There are indeed vague traditions of a festival of the Nativity kept at Rome in the time of Bishop Telesphorus, between A.D. 127 and 139; and some of the Christmas observances of the Roman Church are said to be of his appointment. There is a story of a massacre of Christians in the catacombs on the day of the Nativity in some unspecified year between A.D. 161 and 180; and a similar story of a massacre at Nicomedia in the reign of Diocletian, about A.D. 300; but all these stories are too vague, and the earliest mention of them too late, to be at all reliable.

There was a common belief that the Nativity took place on the 25th day of the month; but *which* month was quite uncertain, and there was scarcely a month in the year to which some guesser did not assign it. Clement of Alexandria (before 220) names five dates, in three different months of the Egyptian year, to which various persons assigned the Nativity; and one of these corresponds to the 25th December. There was, in the third century, a common belief that our Lord was born on the day of the winter solstice. This does not seem to have rested on any record or evidence worth the name, but on a fantastic interpretation of some prophetic scriptures; also on a notion that the Annunciation and the Crucifixion were both on the same day of the year, viz. the 25th of March. The apocryphal book called *The Apostolic Constitutions*, written probably towards the end of the third century, represents the Apostles as ordaining that the feast should be kept on the 25th day of the *ninth* month; by which, however, the context clearly shows that December is meant. The learned John Selden, in his treatise in defence of the traditional date (published posthumously in 1661), affirms that in the early Christian ages the solstice was supposed to fall on the 8th of the Kalends of January, that is, the 25th December. This date, however, has not found universal acceptance. A document assigned to about A.D. 243 gives 28th March as the date of the Nativity; and several modern students infer, from the mention of "shepherds abiding in the field", and from arrangements presumed to have been necessary for the census, that it must have been some time between the end of July and the end of October.

Soon after the end of the last great persecution, between A.D. 310 and 320, or as others say, about 336, the Church at Rome definitely fixed on the 25th December as the birthday of the Lord; the "manifestation", i.e. the visit of the wise men from the East, being celebrated twelve days later. For a couple of generations the Eastern Church continued to make the Epiphany festival, on 6th January, include the commemoration of the Holy Birth; but early in the fifth century the Roman use became almost universal.[1]

[1] Traditions vary greatly as to the time when the Roman usage was generally accepted in the East. By one account it was the result of a consultation between Pope Julius I and Bishop Cyril of Jerusalem about A.D. 352; others mention 375 for Antioch and 385 for

There was much to commend this selection of a date. So long as heathenism was in full vigour the ancient Christians were puritanically jealous of anything that might seem like coquetting with idolatry; but, when heathenism was manifestly declining, there was a disposition to adopt such of its usages as were harmless and capable of a Christian interpretation. And it is not easy to blame this disposition. As the Christ-Child coming into the world transfigured it, so that from the day of His advent it was the same and yet not the same, so the old observances, when associated with the memory of His coming, were animated with a new spirit; and what was heathenish became rich with Christian symbolism. Now in December and the beginning of January there were several festivals which were intimately associated with the daily life of the Roman people. First, from the 17th to the 21st December, was the *Saturnalia*, the great Roman holiday in remembrance of the supposed " Golden Age ". One might call it the Feast of Topsy-turveydom; when slaves were allowed for a few days to enjoy the semblance of freedom, were waited upon by their masters, and chose from among themselves a mock king to preside over their revels. Next, on the 22nd, came *Sigillaria*, the Feast of Dolls, when a fair was held, and dolls and other toys, mostly of earthenware, were given to children. Then, on 25th, came *Brumalia*, otherwise *Dies Natalis Invicti Solis*, The Birthday of the Unconquered Sun, when the days began to lengthen after the solstice. This was neither

Jerusalem; while yet another tradition ascribes the adoption of the western date at Jerusalem to Bishop Juvenalis, about 431.

ancient nor very popular; it is believed to have been instituted as late as A.D. 270 or 273, by the Emperor Aurelian, in honour of Mithras, the Persian Sun-god, of which he was an ardent worshipper. It is worth mentioning here that, of all the new religions which sprang up during the decline of the Roman Empire, Mithraism was the purest in its morality, and the only one which came into serious competition with Christianity. Finally came *Kalendæ Januarii*, the New Year's Day, when everybody gave gifts to everybody else (*Strenæ* they were called); connected with which was *Juvenilia*, the special festival of Childhood and Youth.

Surely it was well that all these should be combined in one great Christian feast, and their ancient significance transfigured in the light of the Gospel; so that instead of the old *Saturnalia*, celebrating the vague tradition of a Golden Age for ever past, this feast should celebrate the sure and certain hope of a Golden Age that shall never end. It should afford not a transient and mocking image of freedom, but a pledge of that liberty wherewith the Truth makes free indeed. And so ere long all Latin-speaking Christendom was joyously singing:

> " O! the ever-blessed birthday,
> When the Virgin, full of grace,
> By the Holy Ghost conceiving,
> Bare the Saviour of our race;
> And the Child, the world's Redeemer,
> First displayed His sacred face:
> Evermore, and evermore."

3. COINCIDENT FESTIVALS

Now this newly established Christian festival coincided very nearly with several other festivals in different parts of the world, the spirit of which was dying out with the decay of the old religions. With many of these were associated customs the original meaning of which was already forgotten, and which survived merely through instinctive conservatism. Others obtained a new lease of life, by virtue of a Christian significance imposed upon them. There was the Jewish *Hanuca*, the Feast of the Dedication; the anniversary, not of the dedicating of Solomon's temple, nor of the temple as restored by Zerubbabel, but of its rededication, after it had been polluted by Antiochus and recovered by the valour of the Maccabees. The Jews called it " The Feast of Lights ", and it was usual to burn great quantities of lamps and candles, as emblems of the Light of Truth, rekindled after it had been awhile obscured by the heathen. The very name of it was transferred by the Latin Church to the Feast of the Nativity. How delightfully would this New Feast of Lights remind the pious Israelite, who had learned to recognize the Hope of Israel in the Child of Bethlehem, that the darkness was past, and the True Light was now shining.

In Egypt, and wherever Mithraism had gained a footing, the new festival would coincide—as it did at Rome—with the birthday of the Sun-god. And the northern barbarians—Britons and Saxons and Norsemen—would find it practically coincident with their own Yule, the feast of the winter solstice and of the returning sun. It seems to have been in pagan times, at least in Norway, the special festival of the god Thor. In the *Heimskringla* we read that King Hakon the Good " made a law that the festival of Yule should begin at the same time as Christian people held it; and that every man, under penalty, should brew a measure of malt into ale, and therewith keep the Yule holy as long as it lasted ". This may or may not have been a desirable way of " keeping the Yule holy "; but it was a pagan festival, kept in the pagan way, with merriment and good cheer throughout the northern regions. Yule, be it remembered, was not a single feast-day, but the whole period of midwinter festivity, the special time of joy and devotion to the Giver of fruitful seasons.[1] And thus to South, and East, and West, and North the rejuvenated Yule would speak of the Sun of Righteousness, arisen with healing in His wings.

It may be convenient to remark here that the Roman Calendar, established by Julius Cæsar in A.U.C. 707 (46 B.C.), and retained in general use for above 1600 years, assumed that the true length of the year was $365\frac{1}{4}$ days, and accordingly provided a " leap year " every fourth year. But closer observation showed that this reckoning was inaccurate to the extent of about 3 days in 400 years. And in 1582 Pope Gregory XIII ordained that ten days (5th to 14th) should be omitted from the month of October

[1] There is some uncertainty as to the actual date of the northern midwinter festival, which *may* not have been held in all places at the same time. But however that may have been, its surviving observances were transferred to the Christian feast, in Germany early in the ninth century, and in Norway about the middle of the tenth.

in that year, and that thenceforward three leap years should be dropped in every 400 years. This correction was promptly adopted in all Roman Catholic countries, but elsewhere it was long rejected as " papistical ". It was only accepted by German, Dutch, and Swiss Protestants about 1700, and was not legalized in the British dominions till 1752. In many places it was slowly and reluctantly accepted; and for three or four generations January 5th (after 1800, January 6th) was persistently observed as " Old Christmas Day ". Moreover, the Reformed Calendar, now universal in the West, has never been adopted by the Greek and other Eastern Churches. Accordingly ecclesiastical seasons in Greece, Serbia, Russia, &c., are dated " Old Style ", so that the Eastern Christmas coincides approximately with the Western Epiphany.

4. NAMES OF CHRISTMAS

Something should here be said of the names by which the Birthday Feast was distinguished. In Rome, and throughout the greater part of Latin Christendom, it was " The Feast of the Nativity "; and in Greece *Genethlia*, having the same meaning. The French *Noël* is variously explained: some derive it, through the Provençal *Nadal*, from the Latin *Natalis*, with which the Italian *Natale* and the Welsh *Nadolig* (probably also the Gaelic *Nollaig*) are compared; others trace it through the form *Nowell* to *Nouvelles*, i.e. news. Possibly both may be right; Noël and Nowell may be words of distinct origin, which, being almost identical in sound, have come to be identified in meaning. Another Italian name is *Natività*, which is evidently the parent of the Spanish *Navidad*. The German *Weihnacht* signifies " the holy or consecrated night ", though some irreverent etymologists have punningly derived it from *Wein-nacht*, i.e. wine night, as if it were only a season of Bacchanalian jollity. " Yule " is, beyond all question, the transferred name of a heathen festival, and may be connected with *Iol*, a wheel, with reference to the turn of the season.[1] Our own " Christmas " is formed on the same pattern as Michaelmas, Martinmas, Childermas, Candlemas, &c.; but opinions differ widely as to the origin and meaning of the syllable -*mas*. Perhaps the likeliest derivation is from the Hebrew *mas*, meaning " tribute " or " offering " (see *Deut*. ch. xvi, 10); whence " mass ", French *messe*, Latin *missa*, applied in the unreformed Church to the principal service of the day, to which all others were subordinate.

5. USE OF EVERGREENS

The Feast of the Holy Nativity, as we have seen, rather incorporated than supplanted various heathen festivals; it was therefore only natural that relics of heathen practice should survive as traditional Christmas customs. A well-known letter of Pope Gregory I to Augustine of Canterbury advises him to permit, and even encourage, such harmless popular customs as were capable of a Christian interpretation. One

---

[1] M. Court de Gibelin, in his *Allégories Orientales*, printed at Paris in 1773, is profuse in his learning on the derivation of this word. " Iol (he says), pronounced Hiol, Iul, Jul, Giul, Hweol, Wheel Wiel, Vol &c., is a primitive word, carrying with it the general idea of Revolution;" and he refers to variants in French, English, Flemish, German, Danish, Latin, Arabic, and Persian. He might have added Anglo-Saxon and Cornish.

of the oldest of these, which nowadays seems the most distinctly English of them all, is the decking of houses and churches with evergreens. This was customary at the Roman Saturnalia, and also, by some accounts, among the northern peoples at their midwinter feast. Its origin is lost in the mazes of antiquity; perhaps the likeliest of many wild conjectures is that it was an offer of winter hospitality to the spirits and fairies that were supposed to haunt the leafless woods. Accordingly the custom was that, wherever else the evergreens might be placed, a spray of berried holly should always appear in the window. One of the earliest Christian references to the practice is by Tertullian (A.D. 200–20). In his treatise on idolatry he strongly denounces it: " Let those who have no light, light their lamps daily; let them over whom hell fire is imminent affix to their posts laurels doomed presently to burn; to them the testimonies of darkness and the omens of their penalties are suitable. You are a light of the world, a tree ever green; if you have renounced temples, make not your own gate a temple." Considering that Tertullian was one of those fanatics who positively courted persecution, this seems to favour a statement that has been made on no very good authority, that in a time of persecution Christians were detected by their not adorning their houses at Saturnalia or Kalendæ; and that afterwards they fell back on the heathen custom, ostensibly in honour of the Nativity, but really as a measure of self-defence. However this may have been, the practice was early discouraged by the Church, and to this day in Italy it is little followed. In France it never had any great popularity; and in Spain it was for-bidden by a Church council in the sixth century.[1] But in England and Germany it has been almost universal; we can trace it back to a very remote Christian antiquity; and at least 500 years ago a religious meaning was read into the trees whose foliage was chiefly employed.

6. HOLLY AND IVY

Of these plants it was early remembered that *ivy* had been the badge of the Wine-god, Bacchus; and it was therefore usually banished to the outside of the house, which the holly, bay, yew, and fir adorned within. Many old songs tell of rivalry between the holly and the ivy: here is one which must be as old as the fifteenth century:

" Nay, ivy, nay, it shall not be, ywis,
  Holly hath the mastery as the manner is.
  Holly standeth in the hall fair to behold;
  Ivy stands without the door, she is full sore a-cold.
  Holly and his merry men they dance and sing,
  Ivy and her maidens weep, and hands wring.
  Ivy hath a kybe, she caught it with the cold,
  So may they all have that with ivy hold.
  Holly hath berries as red as any rose,
  The foresters, the hunters, keep them for the doos.
  Ivy hath berries as black as any sloe,
  There comes the owl, and eat them as she go.
  Holly hath of birds a full fair flock,
  The nightingale, the popinjay, the gentle laverock.

[1] Second Council of Braga, A.D. 572 (can. 73). The prohibition applied to the Kalends, and all other times when such decorations were used by the heathen.

Ivy, what birds hast thou?
None but the owlet that cries ' how, how '."

There were some, however, who thought of the feeble
ivy clinging to its needful support as a lively emblem
of human feebleness clinging to divine strength. Some
such thought may have been in the mind of the old
minstrel who sang:

> " Ivy, chief of trees it is,
>   The most worthy in all the town.
> He that saith other doth amiss;
>   Worthy is she to bear the crown.
> Ivy is soft and meek of speech,
>   Against all bale she is bliss:
> Well is he that may her reach:
>   *Veni, coronaberis.*"

But in the minds of not a few the sombre foliage of
the ivy was associated with thoughts of the grave.
The best-known of all ivy songs is that which tells
how

> " Creeping where no life is seen,
> A rare old plant is the ivy green ".

When this thought is predominant, it is only reasonable that the symbol of mortality should be thrust
out from the house, where all the inward adornments
tell joyously of His advent Who " abolished death,
and brought life and immortality to light ".

As the ivy was the coronal worn by the heathen
in honour of Bacchus, so the *holly*, with its sharp
prickles and blood-red berries, was thought to image
forth the Saviour's crown of thorns.   This thought

peeps forth from another old English Holly Song:

" The holly and the ivy, now they are both well grown;
    Of all the trees that are in the wood the holly bears the crown.
    The holly bears a blossom as white as lily flower;
    And Mary, she bore Jesus Christ to be our Saviour.
    The holly bears a berry as red as any blood; ·
    And Mary, she bore Jesus Christ to do poor sinners good.
    The holly bears a bark as bitter as any gall;
    And Mary, she bore Jesus Christ for to redeem us all.
    The holly bears a prickle as sharp as any thorn;
    And Mary, she bore Jesus Christ on Christmas in the morn."

Holly, it was generally believed, was peculiarly hateful to witches. In the west of England it was said that a maiden should adorn her bed with a sprig of berried holly on Christmas Eve; otherwise she might receive an unwelcome visit from some mischievous goblin. In Germany a sprig of church holly, that is, one which had actually been used in church decoration, was regarded as a charm against lightning. In Cornwall it was thought to ensure good luck all the year to its possessor. In the English Midlands the joke was—perhaps still is—that according as " he holly or she holly ", i.e. that with prickly or smooth leaves, is first brought into the house on Christmas Eve, the master or mistress will rule throughout the ensuing year. But usually in Yule-tide folk-song holly is male and ivy female, as in the carol quoted above. In another, of the fifteenth century, holly and ivy contend for mastery thus:

    " Then spoke holly, ' I am fierce and jolly,
        I will have the mastery in landès where we go.'

> Then spake ivy, ' I am loud and proud,
> I will have the mastery in landès where we go.' "

The text is a little uncertain; the latest editor reads
" I am lou'd and prou'd ", i.e. " loved and proved ",
which certainly seems best to suit the context; for
in the final stanza holly kneels in token of submission.

Akin to this is a superstition that holly affords
protection or brings good luck to the men of the
household, and ivy to the women.

In this connection it may be worth while to quote
a holly and ivy song from a MS. in the British Museum
(Addl. 31922), which is ascribed to King Henry VIII,
and was almost certainly set to music by him:

> " As the holly groweth green
> And never changeth hue,
> So am I, ever hath been,
> To my lady true.

> " As the holly groweth green
> With ivy all alone,
> When flowers cannot be seen,
> And greenwood leaves be gone:

> " Now unto my lady
> Promise to her I make,
> From all other only
> To her I me betake."

It would be interesting to know to which of his six
wives this ditty was addressed.

7. LAUREL, ROSEMARY, FIR, ETC.

Of the other evergreens used for Christmas adornment the *laurel* or *bay*, the emblem of triumph, aptly
symbolized the triumph of Humanity as represented
by the Son of Man. In Friesland a carol is sung by
men impersonating the wise men from the East, of
which every line has for a burden the word " laurel ".
A part of it is thus translated:

> " We come walking with our staves
>   Wreathed with laurel:
> We seek the King Jesus, Him that saves,
>   To bring Him laurel, &c."

As the bay tree, the true laurel of the Ancients, is
rather scarce in England, the common cherry laurel
is generally made to do duty for it; sometimes also
Portugal laurel, Aucuba, &c. These are mere sub-
stitutes, and have no symbolism.[1]

Rosemary was thought to be extremely offensive
to evil spirits, and therefore naturally appropriate to
the advent of their Conqueror. There seems also to
have been in the popular mind a fanciful association
between the name of the shrub and that of the Blessed
Virgin. This seems the most convenient place to
mention a custom which obtained at Ripon in the
latter part of the eighteenth century. The choir boys
of the collegiate church brought in baskets of red
apples, in each of which a sprig of rosemary was

---

[1] Box, which is sometimes found among the Christmas evergreens, has no seasonable
significance. Indeed, if the witness of Herrick may be relied on, its decorative use was only
thought legitimate from Candlemas to Easter Eve.

stuck. One of these apples was offered to every member of the congregation, in return for which a small payment of twopence, fourpence, or sixpence was expected.

Yew and *cypress*, notwithstanding their funereal associations, appeared from their exceeding durability fit emblems of that eternal life which is the portion of those who entertain the Christ-Child, not in the house, but in the heart. And the sweet-smelling *fir* afforded a kind of natural incense in honour of the incarnate Deity. Perhaps this thought had to do with the choice of fir as specially suited for church adornment. So A. Cleveland Coxe sings:

> " I know, I know
>   Where the green leaves grow,
> When the woods without are bare;
>   Where a sweet perfume
>   Of the woodland's bloom
> Is afloat on the winter's air:
>   When tempest strong
>   Has howled along
> With his war whoop wild and loud,
>   Till the broad ribs broke
>   Of the forest oak,
> And his crown of glory bowed.

> " I know, I know
>   Where the green leaves grow,
> Though the groves without are bare;
>   Where the branches nod
>   Of the trees of God,
> And the wild vines flourish fair.
>   For a fragrant crown
>   When the Lord comes down

Of the deathless green we braid
   O'er the altar bright,
   Where the tissue white
Like the winter's snow is laid.

  " And we think it meet
   Our Lord to greet,
As the wise men did of old,
   With the spiceries
   Of incense trees,
And hearts like hoarded gold.
   And so we shake
   The snowy flake
From cedar and myrtle fair,
   And the boughs that nod
   On the hills of God
We raise to His glory there."

8. MISTLETOE

And what about the *mistletoe*, which we are apt to regard as the crown of all? Readers of Virgil will remember it as the Golden Bough, by plucking of which Æneas is enabled to descend into hell, and come safely back. The Druids, as is well known, held it sacred, called it " all-heal ", and ascribed to it all sorts of miraculous virtues. It was not only a specific for every disease, but an antidote to every kind of poison. It rendered cattle prolific; and he who bore it was safe from all witchcraft, was able to see ghosts, and to make them speak. This was especially the case if, as rarely happened, it was found growing on an oak tree; it was then solemnly consecrated by a sacrifice of white oxen, and cut from its parent stem by the Arch Druid with a golden knife, special care being taken that it should by no means touch the ground. Ladies, please remember, when Mr. Somebody claims the privilege of the mistletoe, it has not its proper virtue unless it was cut with a golden knife: also, that the extent of the said privilege is measured by the number of its berries, one of which is to be plucked off at every kiss. There was an old jest that " the maid who is not kissed under the mistletoe at Christmas will not be married that year ".

This custom of kissing under the mistletoe seems to be peculiarly English, and no reliable explanation of its origin seems to be forthcoming. It is not unlikely, however, that it may be a survival from a Scandinavian custom of pre-Christian antiquity. The mistletoe was deemed so sacred that if enemies met casually beneath it in the forest they laid down their arms and maintained a truce till the following day. Thence grew a practice of hanging mistletoe over a doorway, the entering by which was understood to imply a pledge of peace and friendship, to be sealed with a friendly greeting. It was, moreover, an invitation to the spirits of the forest, " who would come in a friendly way in the long winter night, bringing good cheer " and security against any possible jealousy of the gods. Others say that the kiss under the mistletoe is a relic of some primitive marriage rite. The ceremonial cutting of mistletoe for medicinal (or more correctly magical) purposes was practised at midsummer. It was thought of as a spirit or god of vegetation in the tree, which could not—or ought not to—

be cut down until the mistletoe was culled. How or when the midsummer rite was transferred to Yuletide does not appear. In Shropshire the mistletoe is associated with the New Year rather than with the Nativity.

Probably because of its Druidical associations, the mistletoe has usually been disallowed in church decorations. There was one remarkable exception. At York Minster it was long customary for a priest ceremoniously to lay a large bunch of it on the altar. This may possibly have been a survival of some pre-Christian usage; or it may have been a symbol borrowed from the Neo-Druidism of the twelfth century; according to which the mistletoe, dependent on the tree, represented the dependence of man on God. In that case the laying of the plant on the altar might symbolize man, or humanity as expressed in the Incarnate Son, becoming an offering acceptable to God. But indeed of all our evergreens there is none richer than this in Christian symbolism. Its medicinal properties, whether real or imaginary, make it a fitting representative of that Tree of Life, the leaves of which are for the healing of the nations; while its mysterious parasitical growth led to its adoption as a lively emblem of the Virgin Birth.

But a still more beautiful symbolism comes to us from the old Norse mythology. Balder, the god of the summer sun, cannot be hurt by anything on the earth or under the earth. But he is hated by the fiend Loki, who notes that the mistletoe grows neither on the earth nor under the earth, but on a tree. By his craft, therefore, Hœder, " the blind old god whose

feet are shod with silence ", slays Balder with a spear
tipped with mistletoe. When all things in earth and
heaven have wept for Balder, he is restored to life
by Freyja, the goddess of love; whose tears become
the pearls of the necklace Brising, or by another
version of the legend the pearly berries of the fateful
plant. Therefore it was decreed that the mistletoe
should be sacred to Freyja so long as it was neither
on the earth nor under the earth, for which cause it
must always hang on high.[1]

What could be more natural than to adopt the
spirit of this old fable from a Christian point of view,
and to accept the mistletoe as the emblem of that
Love which is stronger than death, and to give it
the place of honour on that night when " Mercy and
Truth met together, Righteousness and Peace kissed
each other ". And why should the Mistletoe Bough
be so constantly associated with that gruesome legend
of the Old Oak Chest? Surely its proper significance
is the victory of love over death, not that of death
over love. The weird melody to which the unseason-
able story is usually sung—not so very old after all—
has come to be a regular element in our Christmas
minstrelsy; why should we not sing it to something
like this?

> The mistletoe bough, in the olden time,
> Was honoured in many a sacred rhyme
> By bards and singers of high degree,
> When cut from its place on the old oak tree
> By white-robed Druid with golden knife;
> For they thought it a magical Tree of Life:

[1] Several students of folk-lore maintain that the legend of Balder is of late origin; and some have even found in it traces of Christian influence.

And many a promise and holy vow
Was solemnly sworn on the mistletoe bough.

The mistletoe bough in the Norseman's lay
Told ever of horror, and love's dismay,
When the old blind god, by a sportive blow,
Laid Balder, the beautiful sun-god, low;
Thenceforth it was deemed an accursed thing;
But Love out of sorrow could victory bring,
And the tears of Freyja are shining now,
Like orient pearls, on the mistletoe bough.

The mistletoe bough on the festive throng
Looks down, amid echoes of mirthful song,
Where hearts make music as old friends meet,
Whose pulse keeps time to the dancers' feet,
And eyes are brighter with looks of love
Than gems outshining the lamps above:
And who is she that will not allow
A kiss, claimed under the mistletoe bough?

The mistletoe bough at our Christmas board
Shall hang, to the honour of Christ our Lord:
For He is the evergreen Tree of Life,
Whom the old blind world, amid hate and strife,
Rejected and slew; but He soared above,
Alive from the dead, in the power of Love:
And Mercy and Truth are assembling now,
With Justice and Peace, at the mistletoe bough.

In Yorkshire and Derbyshire, where mistletoe is scarce, a substitute is (or was) provided in the shape of two crossed hoops covered with greenery, and adorned with ribbons and oranges or bright-coloured apples. Sometimes three small dolls were arranged in the middle to represent the Holy Family. This was sus-

D 287

CUTTING THE MISTLETOE IN DRUIDICAL DAYS

From the painting by Henri Motte exhibited in the Paris Salon in 1901.

pended in the place of honour, and served all the
purposes of the orthodox " kissing-bush ". It has
been suggested that the " mistletoe of the oak ", to
which such marvellous virtues were ascribed, was not
the familiar *Viscum album* with greenish-white flowers,
which grows freely on apple trees, and occasionally on
poplars, willows, and hawthorns, but very rarely on
oaks, but the closely related *Loranthus Europæus*, with
red flowers, which is usually found parasitical on an
oak, but is not native in England. Wherever either
of these plants is found it is associated with similar
superstitions, even as far to the east as Kamschatka
and among the Ainu in Japan.

9. PLACING AND REMOVING EVERGREENS

Tradition prescribed Christmas Eve as the proper
time for placing the festive evergreens; and in Rutland
it was thought unlucky to bring holly into the house
before that time. A likely explanation of this may be
that, in popular belief, the wood-spirits were tricksy,
and might do mischief if they were invited into the
house before the Christ-Child could hold them in
restraint by His mystical presence. On this topic
more will be said hereafter.

Stow tells us, in his *Survey of London* (1598), that
formerly not only houses and churches, but " the
conduits and standards in the streets were likewise
garnished; among thē which I read that, in the year
1444, by tempest of thunder and lightning, towards
the morning of Candlemas Day, at the Leadenhall,

in Cornhill, a standard of tree, being set up in the midst of the pavement, fast in the ground, nailed full of holm and ivie, for disport of Christmas to the people, was torne up and cast downe by the malignant spirit (as was thought), and the stones of the pavement all about were cast in the streets, and into divers houses, so that the people were sore aghast ".

The mode of arranging the decorative evergreens, both in house and church, must always have varied with individual taste. A humorous account of what seems to have been fashionable about 1712 appears in the *Spectator* of 23rd January in that year. " Our clerk, who was once a gardener, has this Christmas so overdeckt the church with greens that he has quite spoilt my prospect. . . . The middle aisle is a very pretty shady walk, and the pews look like so many arbours on each side of it. The pulpit itself has such clusters of Ivy, Holly, and Rosemary about it that a light fellow in our pew took occasion to say that the congregation heard the Word out of a bush, like Moses." About that time it was customary in London for evergreens to be hawked through the streets. In Gay's poem " Trivia " (1713) we read:

" When rosemary and bays, the poet's crown,
    Are bawled in frequent cries through all the town,
    Then judge the festival of Christmas near—
    Christmas, the joyous period of the year.
    Now with bright holly all the temples strow,
    With laurel green and sacred mistletoe."

It is now usual for decorations to follow, as far as may be, the architectural lines of the building.

As to the removal of the greenery, custom was not uniform. Some thought that as the Christmas holidays ended with Twelfth Night, or at the latest with Plough Monday, the decorations ought to remain no longer. Others regarded the festal season as lasting till Candlemas, the fortieth day after Christmas; when, according to the law of Moses, the Mother of our Lord presented Him in the Temple together with her thank-offering, and Simeon recognized the Holy Child as the long-awaited " Light to lighten the Gentiles ". This latter seems to have been the more general English custom, if we may accept the witness of Herrick, who, under the title " Ceremonies for Candlemas Eve ", writes:

> " Down with the Rosemary, and so
> Down with the Bays and Mistletoe;
> Down with the Holly, Ivy, all
> Wherewith ye dressed the Christmas hall;
> That so the superstitious find
> Not one least branch there left behind.
> For look, how many leaves there be
> Neglected there, maids, trust to me,
> So many goblins ye shall see."

In many places it was a rule that the Christmas evergreens, when taken down, should be left to perish by natural decay; to burn them was very unlucky. In Shropshire, on the other hand, the tradition was that they should be burnt on Candlemas Eve.

10. CHRISTMAS GHOSTS

The mention of goblins reminds us that in many places the " Twelve Days " of Christmas were deemed a peculiarly uncanny time; when witches, ghosts, fairies, and the like, were apt to be abroad on various mischief-making errands. This unpleasant superstition may have had a dual origin. In the howling of the winds and raging storms amid the winter's darkness, men thought they heard the voices of supernatural beings, who were probably malignant. And the spread of Christianity, such as it was, among the rude northern peoples, brought in its train the adoption of the Roman Calendar. Thus the superstitions associated with the end of the Old and beginning of the New Year would gradually be transferred from Hallow-e'en—the Celtic New Year's Eve, and the corresponding Scandinavian date—which fell near about Martinmas, to Christmas and the Kalends of January. So it came about that in Germany and the Slavonic countries Christmas Eve was deemed a favourable time for auguries, as Hallow-e'en was in Scotland within living memory. As to those mysterious beings whose voices were heard in the winter's storms, they were very diversely conceived of, though always as objects of dread. They were " The Wild Hunt ", or " The Raging Host ", or " Gabriel's Hounds ", or " The Devil and his Dandy Dogs ". They were the souls of those who had died by violence, or unbaptized, or under a curse; and Odin, attended by the Valkyries, was their leader. In other places they were ancestral ghosts, the family dead revisiting the old homestead; and in some of the Scandinavian countries it was usual, in this belief, to have a meal spread for the ghosts on Christmas Eve, and to leave the beds for their enjoyment, while the family slept in the straw. In Sweden, and also in Poland, it was usual before supper on Christmas Eve to scatter hay or straw on the floor or on the table—obviously a memorial of the Stable at Bethlehem. But some anthropologists, who would derive all religious observances from a supposed primitive animism, suggest that the custom was designed to establish or confirm friendly relations with the Corn Spirit, and thus ensure a plentiful harvest. In other parts of the north witches and trolls were thought to ride about on bears, werewolves, or broomsticks, so that it was dangerous to be out alone. One version of the story was that the trolls, &c., were on their way to Rastekais, a mysterious palace within the mountain, where they would hold festival for the disappearance of the sun. In Germany the leader of the Host was a woman, called by different names in different places, who was attended by dogs, and who in various ways punished the lazy, and sometimes rewarded the industrious. This reminds one of Milton's " lubber-fiend ", the English " Robin Goodfellow ". In France it was thought that Satan was exceptionally busy on Christmas Eve, trying to tempt worshippers on their way to church. He sent witches and warlocks, hobgoblins and ghosts, especially the ghosts of suicides, to roam around farmyards and lurk near cattle-sheds. Therefore on Christmas Eve all doors of stables, cow-houses, and sheep-pens were securely fastened, and no woman was allowed to enter them on any account. Oxen and asses were indeed secure from harm; but horses were especially exposed to the mischievous attentions of " Le Follet ", the French equivalent of Puck.

The immunity of oxen and asses from the attack of malignant spirits is, no doubt, related to the legend of the ox and ass as attendants at the Holy Nativity. Universally popular as this legend is, it has no foundation in the New Testament, nor in any ecclesiastical writer earlier than the year 400. It seems to be based on a strange mistranslation or misreading in the Greek version of *Habakkuk*, ch. iii, 2, where, instead of " in the midst of the years make (it) known ", we read " Between two beasts Thou art made known ". In Hebrew the two phrases are so similar in appearance that, if badly written, one might easily be mistaken for the other. Now in *Isaiah*, ch. i, 3, we read, " The ox knoweth his owner, and the ass his master's crib "; and with this the misread passage about the " two beasts " has been associated. And so in an apocryphal gospel of the fifth century we read, " The most blessed Mary went forth out of the cave, and, entering a stable, placed the Child in the stall, . . . and the ox and the ass, having Him in their midst, incessantly adored Him ". [*Pseudo-Matthew*, ch. xiv.] A literal fulfilment was thus invented for an imaginary prediction: but it is with real regret that we give up the tradition which tells that

> " Ox and ass before Him bow;
> And He is in the manger now."

In Poland and Livonia the unseen terrors of Christmas Eve were werewolves and vampires. In Greece they were " the Kallikantzaroi ", hideous monsters from the underworld, half-human, half-bestial, who went about by night doing all kinds of wanton mischief, and were not completely exorcized until Epiphany, when the priest sprinkled the house with holy water. It is evident that in all this there is very little but pure heathenism.

11. CHRISTMAS TALES

Notwithstanding these imaginary terrors, Christmas has long been accounted, in England at least, the most fitting season for ghost stories. Why this should be the case is a question that leads us into another interesting region of folk-lore. The proverb " Talk of the devil and he'll appear " embodies what was once an established article of belief; that to talk of malignant beings was to invite their approach, and perhaps give them power to do mischief. Yet there has always been a hankering to hear what might be told or dreamed about " the night side of nature "; and perhaps the possibility of danger may have whetted the edge of curiosity. It seems usually to have done so, from the days of Eve and the Serpent to those of Bluebeard and Fatima. But it was felt that the powers of darkness must be helpless in the presence of the Christ-Child. Moreover in the Middle Ages, and far back into the mists of Christian antiquity, there was an idea that the events commemorated in the great Christian anniversaries were mystically repeated at those holy seasons.

So the Saviour was thought of as actually born at Christmas, manifested to the nations at Twelfth-tide, presented in the temple at Candlemas, fasting and tempted in Lent, triumphing on Palm Sunday, crucified on Good Friday, rising from the dead on Easter Sunday, ascending to heaven on Holy Thursday, sending down the Spirit at Pentecost: not literally, of course, but mystically, in such wise that the grace and power of those His saving deeds were specially localized, so to speak, in the corresponding anniversaries.

When we put these two beautifully poetic thoughts together, we understand somewhat of the fitness of Christmas-tide for conversation about the shadowy side of the universe of being. At other times there might be danger in talking too familiarly of " fiends, ghosts, and sprites that haunt the nights "; but at Christmas the power of malignant spirits was so neutralized by the mystical presence of the Christ-Child that curiosity respecting them might be safely indulged. It is to this that Shakespeare alludes where he tells us that:

> " Some say that ever 'gainst that season comes
> Wherein our Saviour's birth is celebrated,
> The bird of dawning singeth all night long:
> And then, they say, no spirit dare stir abroad;
> The nights are wholesome; then no planets strike,
> No fairy takes, nor witch hath power to charm,
> So hallowed and so gracious is the time."

Another tradition, which may well be counted as a Christmas tale, has to do with the gods of heathenism. The early Christians had no doubt of their real existence, not as gods, but as evil demons; and even earlier than the first clear mention of Christmas we find a widespread belief that at the Advent of the Saviour there was a general collapse of the infernal dynasty. It was said that the demons whom the heathen had worshipped as gods were then revealed in their true character, and the oracles which they formerly inspired became silent. Whether these oracles were in all cases pure imposture, or whether belief in them was grounded on obscure facts analogous to the alleged phenomena of modern spiritualism, is a question about which it seems prudent to be less dogmatic than were the men of the last generation. But however this may be, in Egypt, Greece, Italy, and elsewhere, the oracles had been accepted with unquestioning faith from time immemorial. In the age of the Cæsars they began to be regarded with some degree of scepticism; while the Christians generally thought of them as real, but of diabolical origin. This opinion, together with a belief that they became unresponsive at the birth of Christ, survived until quite recent times. The words of Milton on this topic are well known:

> " The Oracles are dumb;
>   No voice or hideous hum
> Runs through the archèd roof in words deceiving.
>   Apollo from his shrine
>   Can no more divine,
> With hollow shriek the steep of Delphos leaving.
>   No nightly trance, or breathèd spell,
> Inspires the pale-eyed priest from the prophetic cell.
>
> .   .   .   .
>
>   " Peor and Baälim
>   Forsake their temples dim,

With that twice-battered god of Palestine;
      And moonèd Ashtaroth,
      Heaven's queen and mother both,
Now sits not girt with tapers' holy shine:
      The Libyc Hammon shrinks his horn;
In vain the Tyrian maids their wounded Thammuz mourn.

     " And sullen Moloch, fled,
      Hath left in shadows dread
His burning idol all of blackest hue;
      In vain with cymbals' ring
      They call the grisly king,
In dismal dance about the furnace blue;
      The brutish gods of Nile as fast,
Isis, and Orus, and the dog Anubis, haste.

     " Nor is Osiris seen
      In Memphian grove or green,
Trampling the unshowered grass with lowings loud;
      Nor can he be at rest
      Within his sacred chest;
Nought but profoundest Hell can be his shroud;
      In vain, with timbreled anthems dark,
The sable-stolèd sorcerers bear his worshiped ark.

     " He feels from Juda's land
      The dreaded Infant's hand;
The rays of Bethlehem blind his dusky eyn;
      Nor all the gods beside
      Longer dare abide,
Nor Typhon huge, ending in snaky twine:
      Our Babe, to shew his Godhead true,
Can in his swaddling bands control the damnèd crew."

All these are tales of the olden time. But there is
another class of Christmas tales which cannot be

altogether ignored. For many years past almost every popular serial has honoured the festal season by a " Christmas number ", consisting for the most part of seasonable fiction. A very large proportion of these tales are of reconciliation of estranged kinsfolk, recognition of long-parted friends, return of errant sons or daughters, forgiveness of injuries, enmity subdued by the return of good for evil, or greed and selfishness expelled from the heart by the hallowed memories of the time. Some few of these, like the immortal *Christmas Carol* of Dickens, have a permanent place in literature; but most of them are too plainly written to pattern, and are sadly lacking in originality. Nevertheless, the motive is usually commendable, and the feeblest of them are generally instinct with the true spirit of Christmas.

12. CHRISTMAS MUSIC—THE WAITS

From Christmas Tales the transition is natural to Christmas Music; and first of the Waits. But let not that honourable title be abused by applying it to Weary Willie and others of the professionally unemployed, who make hideous the long December nights with wheezy clarionets, asthmatic trombones, and fiddles that sound as if their catguts were tormented with the colic. The best things become the worst in their degradation and abuse; and these nocturnal horrors are a counterfeit, or a degenerate survival, of an ancient institution which one would rejoice to see restored to its pristine dignity.

There is some doubt as to the origin of the name

of " Waits ". Some derive it from " wayte ", said to be the ancient name of a musical instrument now called oboe or hautboy. Others say the term originally had nothing to do with music, but merely designated the Town Watchmen. By the beginning of the eighteenth century these had, in some places, become the Town Musicians, to whom the term " the Waits " is applied in *The Tatler*. Until about the year 1820 there were in the cities of London and Westminster companies of " Waits ", whose leaders held office by virtue of some kind of public appointment, and who claimed an exclusive right to solicit contributions from the public.

On the whole, the word seems most naturally to refer to watching and waiting, and may remind us that of old Christmas began in the evening; " The evening and the morning (not the morning and the evening) were the first day ". And when the beautiful thought was cherished of a mystical reiteration of the Holy Nativity at every Christmas-tide, the night that ushered in the happy Birthday was a Vigil, or Watch-night. Who would care to sleep, if perchance he might hear, as did the shepherds of Bethlehem, the herald angels proclaiming the Advent of " a Saviour, which is Christ the Lord "? We may not hear that heavenly music, but we may welcome the jubilant " Gloria in excelsis " of Mozart, rendered with true artistic feeling by a well-practised band; or the solemn strain " O come, all ye faithful " pealing across the snow. Who does not love to hear a choir of youthful voices caroling the blithe old macaronic " Good Christian men, re-joice ", or the sweet minor melody of " The moon

shines bright "? Or who that has spent a Christmas
in Lancashire or Yorkshire has not pleasant memories
of the ever-welcome chorale:

> " Christians, awake, salute the happy morn
> Wherein the Saviour of the world was born."

13. OLD CHRISTMAS HYMNS

Within the century which saw the Christmas anniversary fully established, two great Christian poets vied
with each other in producing *hymns* for its due celebration.   First in order of time was Ambrose, the
brave bishop of Milan, who so reluctantly accepted
the office to which he was called by popular acclama-
tion, but who, when once he was installed therein,
showed that he feared not the face of man by repelling
the great Emperor Theodosius from the Lord's Table
until he showed penitence for innocent blood which
in his anger he had caused to be shed. The Christmas
hymn of St. Ambrose, " Veni Redemptor gentium "
(" Redeemer of the nations, come "), is to be found
in a few recent hymn-books of the " High-church "
type, but it is not suited to modern taste.   Better
known, and far better adapted for social worship, is
the hymn of his great contemporary Prudentius, beginning " Corde natus ex Parentis " (in English " Of
the Father's love begotten "); this has found acceptance, with its fine mediæval tune, among all schools
of religious thought except Unitarians.   These two,
probably the first Christmas hymns ever written, were
part of the ancient heritage of the English Church;
and, with many other good things, were discarded at

the Reformation, not because they were unworthy to
be retained, but because King Henry's new bishops
could not find anybody capable of translating them
into decent singable English. They are still used in
the original Latin in the Church of Rome; as are two
other fine Christmas hymns, " A solis ortus cardine."
(" From lands that see the sun arise "), by Sedulius,
said to have been an Irishman; and " Jesu Redemptor
omnium " (" Jesus, Redeemer of us all "), of uncertain
origin, but probably of equal antiquity. But notwithstanding the habitual use of these hymns in the Roman
Church for nearly 1500 years, none of them, except
that of Prudentius, can be said to have become popular.
The reason is that they are too theological; they are
orthodox divinity in metre, hymns for students or for
the clergy rather than for the people. The same is
true of all, or nearly all, the Christmas hymns of
earlier date than the twelfth or thirteenth century.
Such is the fine hymn of Venantius Fortunatus,
" Agnoscat omne sæculum " (" Let every age and
nation own "), which was regularly used at York
before the Reformation. It is true of a hymn of the
great schoolman Abelard, and of another by his great
antagonist Bernard. No one who sings Bernard's
immortal " Jesus, the very thought of Thee " can
think that its author was lacking in devout emotion;
but when he tried to write a Christmas hymn he only
produced a rhyming tract on the prophecies that were
fulfilled in the Incarnation, ending with a rebuke of
the Jews for not understanding them.

It was just the same in the East. The first hymn
that is sung at the Christmas morning service in the

Greek Church was written by Cosmas of Jerusalem, who died about A.D. 760. It is to my mind very beautiful, but it could never be popular except in the college or the cloister. Here it is, as translated by Dr. J. M. Neale:

> " Christ is born, tell forth His fame!
>   Christ from heaven, His love proclaim:
>   Christ on earth, exalt His name.
> Sing to the Lord, O world, with exultation;
> Break forth in glad thanksgiving, every nation.
>   For He hath triumphed gloriously!
>
> " Man, in God's own image made,
>   Man, by Satan's wiles betrayed,
>   Man, on whom corruption preyed,
> Shut out from hope of life and of salvation;
> To-day Christ maketh him a new creation,
>   For He hath triumphed gloriously.
>
> " For the Maker, when the foe
>   Wrought His creature death and woe,
>   Bowed the heavens, and came below;
> And, in the virgin's womb His dwelling making,
> Became True Man, our very nature taking,
>   For He hath triumphed gloriously.
>
> " He, the Wisdom, Word, and Might,
>   God, and Son, and Light of Light,
>   Undiscovered by the sight
> Of earthly monarch, or infernal spirit,
> Incarnate was, that we might heaven inherit;
>   For He hath triumphed gloriously."

All these hymns are theological; if they mention the *incidents* of the Holy Nativity it is only to emphasize the wonder of the divine condescension; there is absolutely nothing of the homely sentiment of our modern Christmas verse. In a word, they are hymns of the cloister, not of the home.

And this, indeed, is all of a piece with the Christology of the early and middle ages; alike in hymn, and sermon, and treatise, the thought of Christ as Saviour was quite subordinated to that of Christ as King and Judge. Nor can we wonder at this. The sort of government with which men were familiar in those days was mere despotism, which might be wise and benevolent, but was more often selfish, capricious, and cruel. The purpose of Redemption was therefore, so men thought, to substitute for this a Kingdom of God, not less despotic, but perfectly wise, just, and benevolent. And such was the wretched state of mankind during the break-up of the Roman Empire, that to bring home to the minds of men the thought that, in spite of appearances, the universe *was* subject to an omnipotent ruler, perfectly wise, and just, and good, was a real salvation.

So long as the public services of the Church were in an unknown tongue, there was no place for hymns in the vernacular. There was devotional poetry in plenty, but always individual in sentiment and expression. Only after the Reformation did congregational singing form a part of the usual public worship; and even then, in the Calvinistic division of the Reformed Church, the service of praise was long restricted to metrical psalms. Hence we have few if any French hymns of the Huguenot period adapted to ecclesiastical seasons. It was otherwise where Lutheran influence prevailed, and the sixteenth and seventeenth centuries yielded many fine Christmas hymns in the German language. Probably the best-known of these, at least to English readers, is that of Gerhardt, " Fröhlich soll mein Herze springen "—in English " All my heart this night rejoices ". The earliest English pieces to which the name of Christmas hymns—as distinguished from carols—can be properly applied, are that of Ben Jonson, " I sing the Birth was born to-night ", and that of George Wither, " As on the night before the blessed morn ". With the later development of Christmas church-song we are not here concerned.

14. CHRISTMAS CAROLS

From hymns we naturally pass to carols. The distinction is often overlooked; and a chap-book containing, say, thirty " Hymns and Carols ", so called, may include half a dozen true carols, the rest being made up of hymns, pious ballads, and sentimental or festive songs more or less fitted to the season. A hymn is essentially devotional; a carol, in the modern sense of the term, is a song in which a religious topic is treated in a style that is familiar, playful, or festive. The word " carol " originally meant a dance, especially a ring-dance,[1] accompanied with singing, like that of children, " Here we go round the mulberry bush ". We have a classical example of this use in Chaucer (*Romaunt of the Rose*, lines

[1] The derivation of the word Carol has been the theme of much learned discussion. Its remote origin is usually traced from the Greek word *Choros*—the singing and dancing part of a Greek tragedy—through such intermediate forms as the Latin *Chorus*, *Chorea*, Italian *Choreola* and *Carolle*. But one John Palsgrave, in a French dictionary published about 1530, derives the word from Anglo-Saxon *Kyrriole*, which must be derived in turn from the Greek *Kurios*, Lord. Some have suggested derivation from the Welsh *Carawl*; but the Welsh seems more likely to have been borrowed from the English.

793–804). The poet comes upon a bevy of ladies dancing:

> " Upon the karolle wonder faste
> I gan biholde, til attè laste
> A lady gan me for to espie,
> And she was cleped Curtesie.
> Full curtisly she callèd me:
> ' What do you there, beau sire?' quod she;
> ' Come, and if it lykè yow
> To dauncen, dauncith with us now.'
> And I, withoutè tarrying,
> Wente into the karolyng."

Gradually the meaning changed, so as to denote a merry song with a tune suggestive of dancing. In the *Promptorium Parvulerium*, a curious English-Latin vocabulary written about 1440, we find " Carol, songe, palinodium "; another copy gives as the equivalent " Psalmodium, psalmodinacio ". Agreeably to this we read in Spenser's *Epithalamion*:

> " Hark how the cheerful birds do chant their lays,
> And carol of love's praise."

The earliest metrical composition to which the term " carol " has been applied in England, and which is at all related to Christmas, is in the Anglo-Norman dialect of the twelfth century. It has no religious allusions of any kind, and is in fact a mere drinking - song; " Lordings, Christmas loves good drinking " is a typical line. That Christmas was a time specially suitable for merry songs was universally recognized; it was also remembered that it was primarily a religious anniversary; it seemed

natural, therefore, that the merry songs of the season
should embody some religious element. We do not
dance to our carols nowadays; but nothing deserves
to be called a carol which does not tell its sacred
story in a mirthful strain, suggestive rather of the
dance than of the closet or the church.

It is a curious fact that Christmas is the only
festival for which carols have been not only written,
but kept in use. Thus it came to pass that in several
French dictionaries " carol ", defined as above, is interpreted *Chanson de Noël*, i.e. a Christmas song. Yet
there have been good carols written for other seasons,
but nobody sings them, it is hard to say why.
Somehow it has come about that in England we
have so dissociated religion from mirth that they can
only shake hands about once a year. It is well if
then even custom compels us to recognize that the
religion most in harmony with the season is of a
healthy all-round type, which hallows the whole circle
of life, trade, literature, politics, recreation; which
takes up the right old Hebrew carol and sings, " Praise
God with psaltery and harp, praise Him with tim-
brels and dances, and let everything that hath
breath praise the Lord ".

15. ORIGIN OF CAROLS

For eight hundred years and more men had kept
Christmas without carols, unless indeed the term be
applied to Yule-tide drinking-songs; and when at
length these welcome aids to cheerful piety were
produced, it was in connection with a great religious

revival. The birth-place of the true carol was Italy, and its originator, indirectly if not directly, was St. Francis of Assisi—that eccentric genius in whose blended mirthfulness and asceticism, prophetic fervour and childish simplicity, the heart of Christendom has been compelled to recognize that heavenly wisdom which is content to be accounted folly for Christ's sake. We cannot here narrate the strange life-story of St. Francis; it must suffice to say that the original friars whom he gathered around him early in the thirteenth century were the means of the greatest religious revival that had ever been known in Western Europe.

In those days religion was at a very low ebb; the state of society was very rude, and that of morals deplorable. The services of the Church were conducted in a language the people did not understand; the Bible was locked up in an unknown tongue, and had it been otherwise few could have read it; and preaching was unusual and uninstructive. Francis and his friars preached homely sermons full of homely illustrations; and, defective as his gospel might be, it was the power of God unto salvation to multitudes in many lands. It is only within living memory that Francis has come to be understood in Protestant communities; until lately men thought of little but his eccentricities, and the corruption of the *later* Franciscans. It was forgotten that in his day Christ was thought of chiefly as the Awful Judge; the Saviour was almost lost sight of in the " King of Majesty tremendous "; Francis revealed Him as the " Little Brother " of mankind as well. " The Child Jesus " (says Thomas of Celano) " had been given over to forgetfulness in the hearts of many, in whom, by the working of His grace, He was raised up again through His servant Francis ".

There is no evidence, nor indeed any likelihood, that Francis himself wrote carols; but some of his comrades devised an instrument better adapted than even preaching to diffuse religious knowledge among the common people. They composed, in the vulgar tongue, bright homely songs on the great facts of the gospel; and thus, nearly a hundred years before Dante gave stability and literary form to the Italian language, the Italians were singing in the festive strains of the early friars the praises of the Child of Bethlehem.

Several carols of remarkable beauty and tenderness are ascribed to Jacopo da Todi (otherwise called Jacopone), a Franciscan poet of the latter part of the thirteenth century. He is best known as the author of two Latin hymns, each beginning " Stabat Mater "; one of them, the " dolorosa ", probably the most pathetic poem in all ecclesiastical literature; the other, the " speciosa ", though not a carol, having so much in common with our best carols as fairly to demand recognition in this place.

Here is an Italian carol of the same period. The author is unknown; but the tune is almost universally familiar, being the theme on which Handel has built up the ever-welcome " Pastoral Symphony ".

" In Bethlehem is born the Holy Child,
On hay and straw in the winter wild:
Oh! my heart is full of mirth . . . at Jesus' birth.

" They sing aloud in heaven, ' The Child is born,
    Glory to God, and peace on earth forlorn:'
        Oh! my heart, &c.

" Already shines the star, His advent-light,
    It shines above the Child by day and night:
        Oh! my heart, &c.

" First Mary greets the Child in worship true,
    Wraps Him in swaddling-clothes, and loves Him too:
        Oh! my heart, &c.

" The Joseph lowly bows with reverence due,
    And clasps Him in his arms, and loves Him too:
        Oh! my heart, &c.

" The shepherds come upon the Child to gaze,
    And worship Him with songs and sounds of praise.
        Oh! my heart, &c.

" The mage-kings follow soon, the Child to greet,
    Offering gold, and myrrh, and incense sweet:
        Oh! my heart, &c.

" Let us adore the Child this Christmas-tide,
    And offer Him our hearts and souls beside:
        Oh! my heart is full of mirth . . . at Jesus' birth."

From Italy the carol passed over to Spain, France,
and Germany, everywhere retaining its essential character of childish simplicity, religious fervour, and genial
mirthfulness. Some of the old carols are very quaint,
introducing not only legendary matter but pious fiction,
sometimes humorous. One old French carol, of great
length, is curiously dramatic. Joseph and Mary,
arriving at Bethlehem, are, on various pretexts, or

without reason assigned, refused admittance at several inns. At length a hostess, perceiving that Mary is in distress, is about to make provision for her necessities, but is roughly forbidden by her ungracious husband, whom she dares not disobey. Once more repelled, Joseph finds shelter in a stable, where the promised Child is born.

An interesting group of old German carols is that wherein the singer represents himself as accompanying the shepherds in their visit to the Holy Family, and addresses Mary and Joseph in the homeliest as well as the kindliest fashion, and sometimes in the broadest of dialect. Probably the best known and best loved of all German carols is that written by Luther for his little son Hans in 1540: " From heaven above I come to you, To bring you tidings good and true ". The tradition is that in Luther's household the first five verses were sung as a solo, the singer personating the Angel, and the remainder in chorus.

One very curious group, of which specimens in several languages are scattered throughout the southwest of Europe, introduces gipsies in connection with the Nativity. In an Andalusian carol the " rascally gipsies " have stolen the swaddling clothes, and have not left the Child a single rag. In a Spanish carol the gipsies at the town gate welcome the three kings, i.e. the wise men from the East, with a dance. In a Provençal carol the mage-kings are themselves gipsies, who read the lines on the hands of the Child, of Mary, and of Joseph, and predict their several destinies. While in an Italian carol a gipsy woman offers hospitality to the Holy Family during their retreat to Egypt. These odd fancies were probably an outgrowth of the belief, long widely entertained, that the gipsies were exiled Egyptians.

The " Noëls " are a peculiar group, of which we have examples both in French and English, in which the word " Noël " or " Nowell " is oftentimes repeated, generally as a refrain, and evidently in the sense of " news ". The English specimen, " The first Nowell an angel did say ", is too well known to need quotation.

The original purpose of carols required that they should be in the vernacular. But the mediæval clergy were, as a rule, fairly familiar with Latin, and it was only to be expected that some of them would compose Latin carols. Some of these became widely popular, such as: " In hoc Anni circulo " (" In the ending of the year "); " Dies est Lætitiæ " (" Royal day that chasest gloom "); " Resonet in laudibus " (" Faithful souls your praises bring "). But still more widely popular were the Macaronics, in which the language is mixed, part being in the vernacular and part in Latin. Of these there are French, German, and English examples. The original of the familiar " Good Christian men rejoice " is of this class, part Latin and part German, thus: " In dulci Jubilo, Nun singet und sey froh, &c.". The celebrated Boar's Head Carol, of which more anon, is an English Macaronic. Here are a few verses of another, of which in the original the lines are alternately Latin and German:

> " A Child is born in Bethlehem;
> Rejoice therefore, Jerusalem.

" Low in a manger lieth He,
Whose kingdom without end shall be.

" The ox and ass that near Him feed
Know that the Child is Lord indeed.

" From Seba come the duteous kings,
One gold, one myrrh, one incense brings.

" In this, the time of Christmas joy,
To bless the Lord be our employ.

" All glory, Lord, to Thee be done,
Now seen in flesh, the Virgin's Son."

16. THE OLDEST ENGLISH CAROLS

The earliest known copy of an English carol is a fragment published by Ritson, and written, probably, about A.D. 1410:

" I saw a sweet, a seemly sight,
A blissful burd, a blossom bright,
    That mourning made and mirth among:
A maiden mother meek and mild
In cradle keep a knave child,
    That softly slept; she sat and sung,
        Lullay, lulla balow,
        My bairn, sleep softly now."

This very old stanza is valuable as illustrating some well-marked features of our best old English carols. The alliteration is characteristic of the time when it was written. But notice the homely simplicity of the strain; the Blessed Virgin sings just such a lullaby as might have been sung by any English mother in the year 1410. Then see how the whole scene is

treated as if literally present; just what has been said
above about the great events of sacred history being
mystically repeated on their anniversaries. And observe how the whole is brought into personal relation
with the singer; not the bare historic " there was ",
but the personal " I saw ". The true carol is not
the product of an age of cold historic criticism; it
belongs to an Age of Faith.

There is in existence an old MS. song-book, con-
siderably more than 400 years old, supposed to have
belonged to a professional minstrel. From this a
great number of genuine carols were edited for the
Percy Society; some of them, it may be, handed
down by tradition from a time earlier than the Ritson
fragment. It would be pleasant, if space permitted, to
reproduce about a dozen of these, and point out their
most interesting features. This is impracticable; so
we must be content to take a few stanzas here and
there, which show how the old minstrels treated the
leading incidents of the Holy Nativity. First, of the
Annunciation:

> " Gabriel, that angel bright,
> Brighter than the sun's light,
> From heaven to earth he took his flight:
>
> " At Nazareth, that great citie,
> Before a maid he kneel'd on 's knee,
> And said, ' Mary, God is with thee:
>
> " ' Hail, Mary, full of grace;
> God is with thee, and ever was,
> And hath in thee chosen a place, &c.' "

We have not found among the oldest carols any reference to the occasion of the journey to Bethlehem. In one which probably belongs to the early part of the seventeenth century we find:

> " To Bethlehem city in Jewry it was
> That Joseph and Mary together did pass,
> All for to be taxèd with many-one mo';
> Great Cæsar commanded the same should be so.

> " But when they had entered the city so fair,
> A number of people so mighty was there
> That Joseph and Mary, whose substance was small,
> Could find in the inn there no lodging at all.

> " Thus they were constrained in a stable to lie,
> Where oxen and asses they used for to tie:
> Their lodging so simple they held in no scorn,
> And against the next morning our Saviour was born."

The mystery of the Miraculous Birth is dwelt on in these old ditties with considerable *naïveté*. It is not easy to find a quotable stanza on the subject; perhaps this, from the old minstrel's MS., is the most presentable:

> " Blessed be that lady bright
> Who bare a Child of great might
> Without grief, as it was right,
>   Maid Mother Mary.
> God's Son is born,
>   His mother was a maid
> Both after and beforne,
>   As the prophet said,
>   With ay, ay, ay,
> A wondrous thing it is to see
> How maid and mother one can be:
> There was never none but she,
>   Maid Mother Mary."

Another, from a MS. written about 1450, is worth quoting:

> " I sing of a maiden that is makeless (i.e. mateless);
> King of all kings to her Son she ches (?chose).

> " He came all so still to His mother's bower
> As dew in April that falleth on the flower.

> " Mother and maiden, was never none but she:
> Well may such a lady God's mother be."

Of the shepherds keeping watch over their flock by night, we have several descriptions; here is one of the quaintest:

> " About the field they piped full right,
> Even about the midst o' the night;
> They saw come down from heaven a light:
> Tirlè, tirlè, so merrily the shepherds began to blow.

> " Of angels came a company
> With merry songs and melody:
> The shepherds anon 'gan them espy:
> Tirlè, tirlè, so merrily the shepherds began to blow."

The shepherds usually find the Holy Child among the ordinary occupants of the stall. The old carolers appear to have accepted in simple faith the legend of the ox and ass already referred to; a legend which has left its impress not only on popular folk-song, but on the religious drama, and on works of art, even on some of a superior order. So the old minstrel sings:

> " Between an ox stall and an ass
> This Child then truly born He was:
> For want of clothing they did Him lay
> In the cratch among the hay."

Of the appearance of the Star, and the journey of the wise men from the East, we have many very spirited descriptions. The wise men are always kings; their names are usually—not always—Gaspar, Melchior, and Balthazar; one is young, one old, and one of middle age; they represent the respective posterities of Shem, Ham, and Japhet, and the youngest is generally a Moor or a Negro. Their gifts to the Holy Child are explained according to the symbolism which we owe to Irenæus and Nazianzen; the gold proclaims His kingship, the frankincense His godhead, and the myrrh His mortality. Perhaps the best verses are these (spelling modernized):

> " Three kings came out of Indian land
>   To see that wondrous Infant bent,
>   With rich presents in their hand;
>   Straightly a star before them went,
>   A wondrous thing it was to see:
>   That star was more than other three,
>   And it held the course to that countree,
>   With aye, aye, I dare well say
>   They did not miss of ready way.

> " When they with that Lady met,
>   They found the Child upon her knee;
>   Full courteously they did her greet,
>   And present Him with giftès three:
>   As King they gave Him gold so red,
>   Myrrh, incense for His Godhead,
>   Of their offering this we read;
>   With aye, aye, I dare well say,
>   They worshipped Him on Twelfth Day."

The slaughter of the children by Herod is a favourite

topic in the carols, and is often treated with the wildest exaggeration, the Innocents being sometimes counted by thousands. At other times the cruelty of Herod is made the subject of the Virgin Mother's cradle-song, as in a very pretty carol printed in 1587:

" Lulla, lulla, lullaby:
  My sweet little Babe, what meanest thou to cry?
  Be still, my blessed Babe, though cause thou hast to mourn,
  Whose blood, most innocent, the cruel king has sworn.
  And lo! alas, behold what slaughter doth he make,
  Shedding the blood of innocents, sweet Jesus, for Thy sake!
  ' A King is born,' they say, which King this king would kill:
  Oh woe, and heavy woeful day, when wretches have their will."

17. LEGENDARY, MYSTICAL, AND MODERN CAROLS

Some of the old carols are very rich in legendary lore, sometimes from the Apocryphal gospels, sometimes from sources which cannot now be identified. There are often comical adaptations of Oriental matters to Western surroundings, as in the famous Cherry Tree Carol, which tree in the original legend is a date palm. Joseph is an old man, walking with his young bride " in a garden gay, where cherries were growing on every spray ". He is troubled with a fit of jealousy, and when Mary asks him for cherries he replies in rude language, suggesting doubts as to the truth of the message which he has had from the angel. But his doubts are soon dispelled, and his jealousy rebuked; for

" Mary said to cherry tree, ' Bow down to my knee,
  That I may gather cherries by one, two, and three.'

The uppermost bough then bowed down to her knee;
' Now you may see, Joseph, those cherries were for me.' "

Joseph asks pardon for his unjust suspicions; and ere
long an angel tells him that " Our Heavenly King "
will shortly appear:

" He shall not be born in house or in hall,
    Nor in the place of Paradise, but in an ox's stall,
    He shall not be wrapped in purple nor in pall,
    But in fair white linen, as usen babies all.
    He shall not be rocked in silver nor in gold,
    But in a wooden manger that resteth on the mould."

The charming simplicity of these lines is inimitable.

In a less widely-known carol, " The Carnal and
the Crane ", the minstrel, who evidently understands
the language of birds, repeats an overheard confabu-
lation bewteen a crane and a carnal—presumably a
carrion-crow (French, *corneille*). They narrate two old
legends, both of mediæval origin. First, the wise men
tell Herod that Christ is born:

" ' If this be true,' King Herod said, ' which thou tellest to me,
    This roasted cock that lies in the dish shall crow full fences
        three.'
    The cock soon freshly feathered was by the work of God's
        own hand;
    And he crew, ' Christus natus est ', in the dish where he did
        stand."

The Holy Family journey toward Egypt; the wild
beasts worship the Child; and He is recognized
and honoured by a husbandman who is sowing
corn:

" ' God speed thee, man,' said Jesus; ' go fetch thy ox and wain,
  And the corn which thou this day hast sown, go, carry it
    home again.' "

The harvest thus miraculously hastened is reaped and
loaded;

" Then there comes King Herod with his train so furiously,
  Enquiring of the husbandman whether Jesus passed by?"

The husbandman replies that " Jesus passed that way
when my seed was sown "; and Herod retreats, thinking it must be " full three-quarters of a year since he
his seed has sown ".

Some of the carols represent the Infant Christ as
predicting His passion; in one of them Mary is weeping at the recital:

" Now peace, Mother, now peace, Mother, your weeping doth
  me grieve,
  For I must suffer this (He says), for Adam and for Eve."

Some carols of the Holy Childhood are not over
reverent; the Withy Carol, for instance, of which
variants are found in Herefordshire and in Ireland.
In this the Child Jesus is insulted by three boys; to
prove His superiority over them He builds a bridge of
sunbeams, on which they attempt to follow Him over
the sea, but fall in and are drowned. For this Mary
chastises Him with a green withy; and He avenges
Himself by a curse on the entire species: " The withy
shall be the very first tree that perishes at the heart."
This is much on the lines of the worst things in the
apocryphal gospels.

In the carol of the Holy Well, which seems to be

of rather later origin, we are on far higher moral ground. The Child Jesus, having asked of His mother if He might go to play, goes " as far as the holy well "; but is repulsed by the other children, " lords' and ladies' sons ", whom He finds there. Mary hears of it, and is angry, and begs Him to

> " ' Take away those sinful souls, and plunge them deep in hell.'
> ' Nay, nay,' sweet Jesus mildly said, ' Nay, nay, that must not be;
> There are too many sinful souls crying out for the help of Me.' "

Of numeral carols, such as the " Twelve Articles ", " Twelve Points ", and the like, little needs to be said: their form is probably due to a fanciful association with the Twelve Days of Christmas; otherwise they would be equally suitable to any other season. The same may be said of " Dives and Lazarus ", " Jacob's Ladder ", " The Boy's Dream ", " The Seven Virgins ", and others, which, without any intelligible reason, are found in Christmas chap-books.

We seem to have no English specimens of the Satirical Carols which are heard in France, especially in Brittany; wherein the singers of one village indulge in seasonable gibes at those of another. But we have carols which seem to have been originally mystical or allegorical, but to be so corrupted by oral tradition as to have become mere nonsense-verses. Such are " Christmas-day in the Morning ", and that class of numeral carols of which the " Seven Joys " is a fair sample.

A mystical or allegorical carol beginning " Lully lullay; The falcon has borne my mate away ", is assigned to the fourteenth century. It contains evident allusions to the altar, the sacrament, and perhaps to some incidents in the legend of the Holy Grail; but the meaning is by no means easy to determine.

A mystical carol of considerable length, and by no means devoid of beauty, is ascribed to John Awdlay, a blind monk of Haughmond Abbey, Salop; the style is that of the early fifteenth century. The following are a few stanzas:

> " There is a flower sprung of a tree,
>   The root thereof is called Jessè,
>   A flower of price;
>   There is none such in Paradise.

> " The seed thereof was Godès Sond (*sic*),
>   That God Himself sowed with His hand
>   In Bethlehem, in that holy land;
>   Amidst her harbour He there her fand;
>   This blissful flower
>   Sprang never but in Mary's bower.
>   .   .   .   .   .   .

> " Angels there came out of their tower
>   To look upon this freshly flower,
>   How fair He was in His colour;
>   And to behold
>   How such a flower might spring in gold.
>   .   .   .   .   .   .

> " I pray the flowers of this countree,
>   Where'er ye go, where'er ye be,
>   Hold up the flower of good Jessè,
>   For your freshness and your beauty,
>   As fairest of all;
>   And ever was, and ever shall."

Happily one of the best of the English mystical

carols has come down to us without serious corruption.
In this the singer personates our Lord; it is the eve
of His marriage with His true love, the Church:

> " To-morrow shall be my dancing day:
>   I would my true love so did chance
> To see the legend of my play,
>   To call my true love to my dance.
>
> " In a manger laid and wrapped I was,
>   So very poor, this was my chance,
> Between an ox and a silly poor ass,
>   To call my true love to my dance."

The incidents of His baptism, fasting, and temptation,
His betrayal and passion, are similarly told:

> " Then down to hell I took my way,
>   For my true love's deliverance;
> And rose again on the third day
>   Up to my true love and the dance.
>
> " Then up to heaven I did ascend,
>   Where now I dwell in sure substance
> At the right hand of God, that men
>   May come into the general dance."

Several of the Elizabethan poets wrote carols of a
more refined character. We have good ones from the
pens of Herrick, Wither, and other poets of the time
of Charles I. But the ascendancy of Puritanism was,
for the time, as fatal to carols as to maypoles. After the
Restoration there were festive songs in plenty, but few
carols. The rustic muse here and there produced
" godly ballads " of the Childhood and Life of Jesus,
some of which, of great length, still do duty for carols

—or did so quite lately—in various places. But " All ye that are to mirth inclined ", " Faithful Christians ", " The Black Decree ", and " Colmans Carol ", though not bad of their kind, have not the artless spontaneity of the true carol. By far the best of the class is the famous song of Nahum Tate, " While shepherds watched their flocks by night ", which has served to keep from oblivion a name that else had deserved to be dragged down to the deepest pool of Lethe by the dead weight of his " new version " of the *Psalms* and his perversions of Shakespeare. But the song is a pious ballad, not a carol; the festive element is lacking, there is no dance in it—unless perchance it be sung to the old rollicking tune of " Nativity ". It forms a kind of transition from the true carols to the hymns of which the Methodist Revival brought forth such a glorious harvest. But who needs to be reminded of " Hark! the herald angels sing ", or " Christians, awake!" or " Angels, from the realms of glory ", or " Brightest and best ", or " It came upon the midnight clear "?

Hone, writing in 1823, gave a list of eighty-five carols which he had collected. Of this he says, " It excludes all that are disused at the present time, nor does it contain any of the numerous compositions printed by religious societies under the denomination of Carols ". Of these about half have appeared in chap-books within the last thirty years: but nine or ten of them are really hymns. When Hone wrote, it seemed as if the singing of carols had almost died out, except in remote country places, extinguished by the utilitarian spirit of the age. " Carols " (he said)

" begin to be spoken of as not belonging to this century." But a new generation arose, which had eyes to see that the past, however faulty, was not wholly bad. Careful editors and enterprising publishers made familiar to the public the best of the old carols, with their proper tunes, as well as translations from alien sources; and modern poets, imbued with the true Christmas spirit, have produced many new carols scarcely inferior to the old.

18. USE OF CAROLS

As to the manner of using the old carols, no doubt it was for the most part domestic; and just as certainly in the old days as in modern times, they were sung in the streets on Christmas Eve or in the early morning —not always in a spirit of pure devotion. Hone, in his *Ancient Mysteries*, p. 90, quotes a curious stanza, which, by its spelling, might seem to be of the fifteenth century, unless indeed it is (as we strongly suspect) a clever modern imitation:

> " The lewid peple than algates agre,
> And caroles singen everi' criste messe tyde,
>   Not with schamfastenes bot jocondle,
> And holey bowghes aboute; and al asydde
>   The brenning fyre hem eten, and hem drinke,
> And laughen mereli, and maken route,
>   And pype, and dansen, and hem rage; ne swinke,
> Ne noe thynge els, twalve daye' thei wolde not."

In the *Every Day Book*, vol. i, p. 800, he says: " These ditties, which now exclusively enliven the industrious servant maid and the humble labourer, gladdened the festivity of royalty in ancient times. Henry VII, in the third year of his reign (1487), kept his Christmas at Greenwich. On the twelfth night, after high mass, the king went to the hall and kept his estate at the table; in the middle sat the dean, and those of the king's chapel, who immediately after the king's first course sung a carol."

As to whether carols were to any great extent substituted for the usual psalmody in church, we are not very fully informed. Certainly Herrick's carols were designed to be sung in the Chapel Royal at Whitehall. At Exeter the various church choirs used to go about singing carols through the night; and then mustered in the cathedral at seven in the morning, where they joined in singing the Old Hundredth Psalm before the usual service. Davies Gilbert, writing in 1822, says that in the west of England, down to the end of the eighteenth century, on Christmas Eve it was customary in many houses to spend the time in carol-singing from seven or eight in the evening till late into the night; the intervals being devoted to the consumption of hot cakes and ale or cider. Then " On Christmas day these carols took the place of psalms in all the churches, especially at afternoon service, the whole congregation joining; and at the end it was usual for the parish clerk to declare in a loud voice, his wishes for a merry Christmas and a happy new year to all the parishioners ".

At many places in Wales a service called " Plygain ", i.e. Dawn, was held at four or five o'clock in the morning. Sometimes the parson was escorted from his house to the church by young men with torches, and

the church was lighted with coloured candles. The
character of the service varied in different places;
sometimes there was celebration of the Holy Communion; sometimes the parson sang the first verse
of a carol, the clerk sang the second, and then carols
were sung round the church in procession. In some
places refreshment was provided in the shape of hot
broth. These services, which seem suggestive of a
survival from the Midnight Mass of pre-Reformation
times, are said to have generally died out in the Episcopal Church soon after the middle of the nineteenth
century. About the same time, it is said, Plygain
services began to be held in Welsh Nonconformist
chapels; but of late they seem to have been more
usual on the morning of the new year.[1] Much akin
to the Welsh Plygain is the custom that prevails in
Norway. There, as in all the Scandinavian countries,
the usual type of religious thought is Lutheran, and
the Midnight Mass is therefore not to be looked for;
but it is replaced by a service called *Julotte*. The
regular time for family gatherings is Christmas Eve;
but in the morning before daybreak the whole parish
assembles in the church for a service of praise, which
consists chiefly of singing. Rows of candles are arranged along the backs of the benches, so that the
church is brilliantly illuminated; and as many Norwegian parishes are of great extent, it is no uncommon
thing to take a journey of several miles to participate
in the " Julotte ". In Lapland the parishes are of
still greater extent, so that the journey to and from

[1] The Welsh language has an ample supply of carols. Hone mentions two volumes, one
containing 66 carols for Christmas, and 5 for summer; the other containing 40 Christmas
carols, 1 for winter, 3 for May, 9 for summer, 1 to the nightingale, and 1 to Cupid.

the church may occupy two or three days. And it is said that the sleigh-ride with its jingling bells is looked forward to by the children for months together.

This seems the most convenient place to mention what is reported from Finland, where every sailor and fisherman endeavours to spend his Christmas at home. Accordingly all boats come into harbour on St. Thomas's Day (21st December), and preparations for Christmas begin. On Christmas Eve everyone takes a hot bath, and the evening is spent in singing hymns and telling stories of adventure. All rise before dawn, and proceed to church—the journey being often of many miles, sometimes over a frozen arm of the sea. Lights are set in the church windows, and a cross is placed over the door, " to show that there is Christmas joy within ". Special holiday fare is given to the cattle, and a sheaf of corn is set upon the roof, that the birds may keep festival.

A very curious custom obtained in several parishes in the Isle of Man. People assembled in the church on Christmas Eve—" Oiel Verry ", i.e. Mary's Eve, they called it: each in turn sung a carol as a solo, holding in his or her hand a lighted candle. The carols were very lengthy; but the singer had to stop if the candle went out. The ceremony ended at midnight.

At Crondall, in Hampshire, until about 1860, carols used to be sung from the top of the church tower. A similar custom still survives in a few towns in Germany, and was formerly much more general. Luther's carol " From heaven above I come to you "

"GOD REST YE MERRY, GENTLEMEN; LET NOTHING YOU DISMAY!"

From the painting by J. Seymour Lucas, R.A.

The artist has chosen as the title of his picture the opening lines of a carol popular during the seventeenth century.

D 287

is the one usually sung, the melody being led by a trumpet or cornet.

Of late years a pleasant custom has grown up, in many places, of church choirs, or glee-parties, perambulating a village or district, singing carols, and collecting donations for some well-understood charitable object. This practice surely embodies the genuine spirit of Christmas, and deserves general imitation.

19. CHURCH OBSERVANCES—ADVENT

Remembering that Christmas is, above all things, a religious anniversary, we turn awhile to the Church observances of the season. From early in the sixth century it has been usual throughout Western Christendom—though not in the Greek Church—to set apart the four Sundays next preceding Christmas as a season of devotional preparation. This was, and still is, known as the season of Advent; and special prayers, anthems, and hymns for the four Sundays and some other days are given in the Church service books. According to the Roman use, and those uses which generally prevailed in England before the Reformation, the *Te Deum* and *Gloria in excelsis* were not sung during Advent; but all the antiphons had a note of expectation, leading up to the " Seven great O's " at Vespers on the seven days preceding Christmas Eve. These have happily been restored to use within the last generation, and their use is by no means limited to the Episcopal Church.

Advent being a preparation for Christmas, as Lent was for Easter, it came to be regarded as in like manner a season of abstinence. So the Roman Church ordained that every Wednesday and Friday of the four weeks should be kept as a fast; and that if marriages took place they should be " without outward pomp or festivity ".   Kirchmeyer tells us that in Germany witches and evil spirits were thought to be especially mischievous on the Thursdays in Advent. On those days children ran about the streets, knocking at every door, and crying, " The Advent of the Lord: a happy New Year ", for which they expected apples or pence. At the same time girls sought by divination with onions and faggot-sticks to learn something about their future husbands.

In Rome, Naples, and other Italian cities, images or pictures of the Blessed Virgin are often placed at street corners and in other public places. It was customary in the eighteenth century, and perhaps is still, for the Calabrian shepherds, during the last few days of Advent, to come into the cities with musical instruments, usually bagpipes, and play before these images and pictures as an act of devotion. They would also play before a carpenter's shop " to show respect to St. Joseph ".

Advent ends with Christmas Eve. It was customary in the papal chapel at Rome that, if a Sovereign Prince were present at Matins on that day, he should read one of the lessons, holding in his hand a drawn sword in token of his readiness to defend the Church. After this custom had become obsolete, the Pope was accustomed on Christmas Day to bless a sword and hat, which were sent as gifts to some royal personage.

In Holland the characteristic observance of Christmas Eve is, or was, of a more democratic type. At midnight the young men of a town or village, some of them in fantastic costumes, meet in the principal square or open space, and after singing *Gloria in excelsis*, or its Dutch equivalent, choose one of their number as Star-bearer. A large lantern has been provided in the shape of a star, containing many candles and mounted on a pole. This is borne at the head of a long procession through every street, the company singing the *Gloria*. The whole effect is said to be very impressive.

A custom existed in Yorkshire which certainly cannot be called a Church observance, but which is most conveniently mentioned here, because it is connected with the season of Advent. The children went about carrying what was called " the Yule Baby ", an elaborately dressed doll in a decorated box, which represented the manger at Bethlehem. Sometimes there were two dolls, to represent the Holy Child and His Mother. It was thought unlucky if any house was not visited by these " Advent Images ". This custom was, in all likelihood, a survival of the mediæval " præsepio ", of which more hereafter.

20. CHURCH OBSERVANCES— CHRISTMAS BELLS

As is well known, according to ecclesiastical usage the day begins at sunset. The evening service on what we now commonly call Christmas Eve was therefore the " First Vespers " of Christmas Day. At such a festive season it was a matter of course that every service should be heralded by the merry chiming of

church bells: and whatever else ultra-Protestantism
and Puritanism have wisely or unwisely swept away,
we may be thankful they have not silenced the Christmas bells. Long and ever louder may they ring out
the joyous invitation:

> " O come, all ye faithful,
>   Joyful and triumphant;
> O come ye, O come ye to Bethlehem:
>   Low in a manger
>   Lies the King of Angels;
> O come, let us adore Him, Christ the Lord."

There is one very quaint bit of folk-lore pertaining to
Christmas bells. At Dewsbury, and no doubt at some
other places, it was customary that the great bell
should toll, as if for a funeral, for an hour before midnight; and as soon as the hour was past the ringers
struck up a merry peal. This seems to have been a
survival of a rather widespread mediæval custom, the
purpose of which was said to be to give the powers
of darkness notice of the approaching birth of the
Saviour. Later it was called " Tolling the Devil's
knell "; for, it was said, " The Devil died when Christ
was born ". It is to be feared that he had a speedy
resurrection; but the saying was a striking, if exaggerated way of presenting the truth that the birth of
Christ gave a death-blow to the empire of Satan. On
this conceit Dr. J. M. Neale wrote a delightful little
poem to an ancient carol tune:

> " Toll, toll, because there ends to-night
>   An empire old and vast;
>   An empire of unquestioned might

O'er present and o'er past;
Stretching wide from east to west,
Ruling over every breast,
    Each nation, tongue, and caste.

" Toll, toll, because a monarch dies
    Whose tyrant statutes ran
From polar snows to tropic skies,
    From Greenland to Japan:
Crowded city, lonely glen,
Ocean, mountain, shore, and fen
    All owned him lord of man.

" Toll, toll, because that monarch fought
    Right fiercely for his own,
And utmost craft and valour brought
    Before he was o'erthrown;
He the lord and man the slave;
His the kingdom of the grave
    And all its dim unknown.

" Joy, joy, because a Babe is born
    Who, after many a toil,
The scorner's pride shall laugh to scorn,
    And work the foiler's foil:
God as Man the earth has trod,
Therefore man shall be as God,
    And reap the spoiler's spoil."

Christmas Bells, in England, are popularly associated with frost and snow. But their music is heard in
southern latitudes, and is as seasonable in an Australian
summer as in an English winter. Here are a couple of
stanzas from a book entitled *The Christian Year under
the Southern Cross*, published in New Zealand:

" No touch of winter's frosty breath,
    No snowclad fields 'neath skies that lower;
All Nature thrills with joyous life,
    As faintly from the distant tower
Ring out the cheerful Christmas Bells.
Hark! how their cadence softly swells
O'er open fields and bosky dells,
    ' In Excelsis Gloria!'

" 'Neath skies of blue the plains lie decked
    In thousand varying shades of green.
Soft shadows sweep o'er meadows gay
    With many a floweret's brilliant sheen;
While Christmas Bells in glad refrain
Sound the glad tidings once again
Which angels sang in raptured strain,
    ' In Excelsis Gloria!' "

It is perhaps scarcely worth while to mention here that in many English villages handbell ringers visit the principal houses about Christmas-time collecting largess.

21. CHURCH OBSERVANCES— MIDNIGHT MASS

Most readers will remember Scott's poetic enumeration of Christmas customs; amongst which he reminds us that

" On Christmas Eve the bells were rung,
On Christmas Eve the Mass was sung:
That only night of all the year
Saw the stoled priest his chalice rear."

Reference to the Roman or Sarum Missal will confirm this statement, provision being made for three masses on Christmas Day, while on no other festival is a midnight mass permitted. The custom was instituted at Rome in the earlier half of the fifth century. The Pope sang the first mass at midnight, at Sta. Maria Maggiore; the second at St' Anastasia; and the third at St. Peter's.

There can be little doubt that " Midnight Mass on Christmas Eve only " originated in a belief that the Birth of our Lord occurred about midnight—a matter about which there is no real evidence one way or the other. The belief had, however, some imaginary support in a pious misapplication of a passage in the *Book of Wisdom* (ch. xviii, 14–5):

" When peaceful silence enwrapped all things,
 And night in her own swiftness was in mid-course,
  Thine all-powerful Word leaped from heaven out of the royal throne,
 A stern warrior into the midst of the doomed land."

This, as the context clearly shows, refers to the slaying of the first-born of Egypt; but mediæval divines applied it to the Incarnation of the Word. Hence a beautiful Latin carol, probably of the fourteenth century, beginning " Quando noctis medium ":

   " When in silence and in shade
    Earth at midnight had been laid,
    Working out the Father's plan,
    In the Virgin's womb made Man,
    God His earthly life began."

It certainly seems fitting that the central ordinance of Christian worship should have a place among the solemnities of the Saviour's birthday; and one of the worst evils that have resulted from the perversion of that ordinance into the Romish Mass is that it has sometimes become a point of orthodox Protestantism to thrust into a subordinate and obscure place what the Apostles and primitive Christians placed foremost.

In Paris, and probably in other French cities, it was usual to proceed direct from the Midnight Mass to a family gathering, where as sumptuous a meal was provided as funds would allow, and where family affairs were discussed, and endeavours made to appease quarrels and put an end to misunderstandings. In Brittany poor old women wait about the church door to take charge of the lanterns which the country folk all carry to light them on their way. After the mass the owners of the lanterns, on reclaiming them, always give substantial alms to the caretakers.

At Madrid people traversed the streets with torches, tambourines, and guitars, and after mass danced in the body of the church.[1] A similar custom existed in the Spanish-American cities. In Sicily the midnight service was often sadly lacking in reverence, downright pagan licence intruding; and it is said to have been much the same in the Rhineland, until Midnight Mass was abolished.

At Rome, at Sta. Maria Maggiore, certain pieces of wood were preserved, which were alleged to be part of the actual cradle of our Lord! These it was usual, within the last century, to bring forth in solemn procession early on Christmas Morning, and after

[1] Dancing in church was very early practised in Spain at several festivals. It was forbidden by a Council at Toledo in 589 or 590; but popular custom was too strong for ecclesiastical authority, and it survived, at least at Christmas, till about 1200. Even to quite recent times (if not to this day), on certain feast days choir-boys with castanets danced before the altar in Seville Cathedral. In York Minster, till the seventeenth century, the choir-boys were accustomed to dance in the nave after morning prayers on Christmas Day. And at Besançon, until 1727, it was usual to dance a "bergette".

AFTER MIDNIGHT MASS, FIFTEENTH CENTURY

From the painting by G. H. Boughton, R.A.

high mass to deposit them on the principal altar.

According to Kirchmeyer it was customary in some parts of Germany, after the third mass, to place on the altar an effigy of the Holy Child, duly wrapped in swaddling clothes; around which the boys and girls would dance and sing carols. A variant of this custom was—perhaps still is—observed in the Church of the Holy Nativity at Bethlehem. At the end of the mass the " Bambino " is placed on the altar, and then carried in solemn procession to the crypt; where it is laid on the silver star in the pavement which is supposed to mark the actual place of the Divine Birth. The narrative is read from the *Gospel of Luke*; and when the reader comes to the words " laid Him in a manger ", the effigy is lifted from the floor and placed in a rock-hewn trough which represents the manger, and which many simple-minded pilgrims believe to be the veritable cradle of the Holy Child. In mediæval England, after matins, a deacon—or the bishop if he were present—chanted the " Genealogy " in *St. Matthew* (chap. i), followed by the *Te Deum*. This custom still survives in some Benedictine churches.

22. NATIVITY PLAYS

Christmas was very early provided with one of those semi-dramatic services which in course of time developed into the Mystery or Miracle Play. In the cathedral at Rouen, in the twelfth century, an image of the Virgin and Child was placed in a stable behind the altar. A boy, placed before or above the choir, and personating an angel, announced the Nativity to certain canons, as they entered below in the character of shepherds. As they passed through the great door of the choir, vested in tunics and amices, many more boys stationed on high began to sing " Glory to God in the highest ", to which the shepherds replied " Peace on earth to men of goodwill ".[1] As they advanced up the choir two priests, clad in dalmatics, and representing women, met them inquiring, " Whom seek ye?" They answered, " Our Saviour, Who is Christ the Lord ". The priests then drew back the curtain, saying " The Little One is here, as said Isaiah the prophet "; they then showed the mother, saying " Behold the Virgin ". On this the shepherds bowed, worshipping the Child and saluting the Mother, and returned to the choir singing " Alleluia ". Thus was the Story of Bethlehem both acted and sung in the mediæval Church.

From such beginnings grew that rich treasury of religious drama which flourished in England from the thirteenth to the sixteenth century, and which still survives on the Continent, at Ober-Ammergau and elsewhere. But the English Nativity Plays were not exclusively, nor even chiefly, associated with Christmas; they formed portions of those great cycles of plays which were acted in the open air on movable stages or " pageants ", by members of various guilds, and usually in the summer-time. It is not necessary, therefore, to treat them at any great length. It may suffice to say that we possess five series of these plays, four English and one Cornish, besides a few detached specimens. The cycles contain from twenty-five to forty-eight

[1] " In terra pax hominibus bonæ voluntatis "; this, the rendering of the Vulgate and the older Latin, as well as of several other very ancient translations, is supported by a majority of the oldest Greek manuscripts of the gospel.

plays apiece, and together they cover the whole field of sacred history, from the Creation to the Final Doom. The treatment of the Nativity may be estimated from the Interlude in Longfellow's *Golden Legend*, if we remember that the modern poet exhibits a refinement which is totally lacking in the rugged originals. A few brief selections may be interesting.

In the York play of the Nativity, Mary thus soliloquizes:

> " Now in my soul great joy have I;
> I am all clad in comfort clere;
>   Blest mote He be.
> Jesu my Son that is so dear,
>   Now born is He.
> Hail, my Lord God! Hail, Prince of Peace!
>   Hail, my Father, and hail, my Son!
> Hail, Soveran Sege, all sins to cease!
>   Hail, God and Man, on earth to wonne!
>   Hail, through whose might,
>   All this world was first begun,
>   Mirkness and Light!"

The Wakefield plays are characterized by a rough humour. The shepherds are grumbling about hard work, poor wages, heavy taxes, cold weather, and termagant wives. They lie down to rest; and while others are sleeping one of them steals a sheep and carries it home, where his wife hides it in the cradle. By and by the shepherds come in quest, and discover the sheep when one of them insists on kissing the new baby—whereupon the thief is punished by being tossed in a blanket. The rest then return to the fold; and, again lying down to sleep, are thus aroused by the angel:

" Rise, herdmen hynde; for now is He born
That shall take fro' the fiend what Adam had lorne:
That warlock to shend, this night is He born!
God is made your Friend; now at this morn
    He behests, at Bedlem go see,
    There lys He in a crib poorly."

There is generally quaint humour in the homely gifts presented by the shepherds. In the Chester play they include a bell, a flask, a spoon, a hood, a pipe, and a nut-hook. But their salutation in the York play is really beautiful:

" Hail! the Fairest of field-folk for to find!
    Fro' the fiend and his feres faithfully us fend;
    Hail, the Best that shall be born to unbind
    All the bairns that are born and in bale bende."

The Coventry plays make much use of apocryphal matter, including the Cherry Tree incident. After the shepherds have presented their gifts, Herod appears, proclaiming:

" I am the mightiest conqueror that ever walked on ground;
    Magog and Madrocke, both these I did confound,
    And in this bright brand their bones I brake asunder,
    That all the world on those raps did wonder!"

He claims to be lord of lightning, prince of purgatory, and chief captain of hell! When he learns that the wise men have gone home another way he vows, if he can catch " those villain traitors ", he will burn them, and forthwith orders all the children in Bethlehem to be slain. The bodies of the children are brought to him in a cart; but, finding that Jesus is not among them, having escaped into Egypt with Joseph and Mary, he " rages in the pageant and in the street ", and gallops off in pursuit.

There are no Nativity scenes in the great Cornish cycle of religious drama; but there are two plays not contained in either of the cycles, which were written by one John Parfre in 1512. One of them is on the Slaughter of the Innocents, the other on the presentation of the Infant Jesus in the temple. In the latter, Simeon " the bishop " speaks a prologue in which he expounds the doctrine of the Incarnation, and prays that he may not die until he has seen the sweet face of the Divine Child. Mary and Joseph enter, and present the Child to Simeon, together with the offering of two young doves; and he, after reciting *Nunc Dimittis*, paraphrases it in sixteen lines of rhyme. Then Anna calls forth a company of young maidens, exhorting them to "worship this Child, very God and Man ". Simeon " bears Jesus in his arms, going a procession round about the temple "; and all this while the maidens sing *Nunc Dimittis*. Simeon returns the Child to His Mother, predicting His crucifixion, and the " sharp sword of sorrow [that] shall cleave her heart atween "; and bids Anna teach those maidens " to please God of most honour ". She at once responds: " Worship we Jesus that shall be our Saviour; all at once come on, and follow me "; and they conclude the performance with a dance.

Crude Nativity plays are still acted in Roumania; and in the middle of last century they were common in Poland, Provence, Naples, and Spain, the characters being sometimes represented by puppets.

Within the last few years Nativity plays, modern in structure and reverent in expression, have been presented at Christmas-tide in several church halls and schoolrooms; and it is not impossible that these may be first steps toward a resuscitation of the religious drama.

23. THE PRÆSEPIO

On Christmas Eve, 1224, a very realistic tableau of the Nativity was arranged by St. Francis in a village church at Greccio in Italy. Joseph and Mary, represented by real persons, watched beside a manger in which a figure of the Holy Child lay upon straw, while a real ox and ass were tethered close by. Mass was celebrated, and Francis preached on the topic of the season. This was the origin of the simple object lesson called the " Præsepio ", or " Presepe ", or popularly " The Christmas Crib "; which with innumerable variations has been reproduced at Christmas in almost every Roman Catholic church in Christendom; and has found its way, with divers adaptations, far beyond the limits of the Church of Rome—as, for example, in the celebrated Moravian School at Neuwied.

A visitor to Rome in the early part of the nineteenth century describes the præsepio in the Church of the Ara Coeli as best worth seeing. Daylight was completely excluded, and the artificial light " was so managed as to stream in fluctuating rays from intervening silvery clouds, and shed a radiance over the Child and His mother, who in a graceful attitude holds up the drapery which half conceals the sleeping Infant ". His swaddling clothes are richly embroidered,

and both He and His mother are adorned with jewels
lent for the purpose by princesses and other ladies
of high rank. " Groups of cattle grazing, peasantry
engaged in different occupations, and other objects
enliven the picturesque scenery; and every living
creature in the group with eyes directed to the præsepio,
falls prostrate in adoration." During the visit thus
described, a little girl of six or eight years old stood
on a bench and recited a suitable discourse " with all
the gesticulations of a little actress; perhaps in commemoration of those words of the Psalmist, quoted
by our blessed Lord, ' Out of the mouths of babes
and sucklings Thou hast perfected praise ' ".

In Southern Italy the " presepe " is a domestic as
well as a Church custom. The manger is constructed
and adorned a week beforehand, and is often a genuine
work of art. C. A. Miles, in *Christmas in Ritual and
Tradition*, reproduces a photograph of a magnificent
Neapolitan " presepe " which represents the Holy
Family in a shed formed amidst the ruins of a Corin-
thian temple. On each side the shepherds approach
with their offerings; one leads a lamb, another is
attended by a dog, others have brought gifts in baskets.
Four or five baby angels are fluttering above. The
ox and ass do not appear in the shed; but below is a
cave, near the entrance of which oxen are standing or
lying. Shepherds are negotiating with a doorkeeper
for the admission of a few sheep into the cave, while
a number of goats are left outside. The whole is built
up in one corner of a lofty hall, of which it almost
reaches the ceiling.

The domestic presepe is often the work of the

children; and in Rome an enormous bazaar, as well as numerous shops, supply materials for its construction. There are earthenware figures varying in price from a halfpenny to many shillings, cork to represent rockwork, moss, and liverwort, and scenery roughly painted in watercolours. For the construction frequently includes not only the stable or cave and its occupants, but the surroundings of Bethlehem, imagined in complete ignorance of geography and history; " an orgiastic medley of chaos and luxuriant riches, a radical negation of all the notions of time and space, this is what the bold Roman boy gathers around the crib, in which after all they sometimes forget to place the Bambino ".

From the first setting up of the presepe till Christmas Eve visits are exchanged, and mutual criticisms are passed on the domestic preparations. Minstrels come round with bagpipes and carols, and sing or recite prayers before every presepe whether in house or church. Then on Christmas morning the Bambino is placed in the manger, with solemn ceremonies, and feasting begins in earnest. In Bohemia the præsepio, or as it is there called " the Bethlehem ", is a permanent memorial " arranged on a tiny stage, and often handed down from generation to generation; and great care is expended in carving, painting, and dressing the figures and keeping them in repair ".

In some parts of France, and perhaps in other countries, the præsepio serves as it were to visualize the belief, already mentioned, of a mystical repetition of the Incarnation at Christmas. This is thought of in relation to the Midnight Mass, at which solemnity

people gather from outlying hamlets *literally* to visit
the Holy Child. Sometimes great store of provision
is brought, nominally as gifts to Joseph and Mary,
really for a picnic after mass, at which the participants
are guests of the Holy Family. This custom gave birth
to a class of curious carols, abounding with local allusions both to persons and places, sometimes compli-
mentary, sometimes sarcastic. No such carols exist in
English; but there can be little doubt that the interesting group of carols, in many languages, which have
the form of a cradle-song sung by the Blessed Virgin
to the Holy Child, were originally associated with the
præsepio.

24. CRADLE-ROCKING: THE POSADA, ETC.

In this connection mention must be made of the
curious custom of Cradle-Rocking (Kindel-wiegen),
which arose in Germany about the fourteenth century,
and long retained its popularity. The crib became a
cradle that could be rocked, at first by priests, who
personated Joseph and Mary, while choir and people
sang and danced around. Then the custom became
domestic, but still a real act of devotion. Some very
pretty German carols relate to this custom, with which
the fine old Latin carols " Quem pastores laudavere "
and " Resonet in laudibus " were also associated. The
practice died out very slowly; it survived at Tübingen
as late as 1830, and to a still more recent time in out-
of-the-way places in Tyrol. In Sicily, especially at
Messina, at least down to the middle of last century,
it was usual on several nights before Christmas to fire

a large number of crackers, as a midnight salute to "the Madonna and her sacred Mother"! Then on Christmas night, i.e. the night following first vespers, the streets were thronged and every house was lighted in honour of the procession of the " caro Bambino ". This commenced at midnight, and was formed by the clergy, municipal bodies, lines of military with music, church attendants, &c., all singing and bearing torches, and followed by a tiny wax doll in the arms of a priest beneath a gorgeous canopy. Fireworks were let off in the streets, and few people went to bed before dawn.

In some of the Spanish-American cities, especially in Mexico, there is a curious domestic custom called the *Posada*, i.e. the Inn, based on a tradition that Joseph and Mary had a nine days' journey from Nazareth to Bethlehem. For the due observance of this custom several neighbouring families—preferably kinsfolk—unite; and on each of the nine evenings from 16th to 24th December they gather in one selected house, the ladies taking in turn to act as hostess and give a present of some kind, however small, to each one of the company. The evening is usually spent in merrymaking, dancing, and a romp with the children. But on one evening of the nine observance becomes distinctly religious. The attendance of a priest is secured, a temporary altar is fitted up in the principal room, and under it is placed the præsepio and its appropriate figures. As midnight approaches the priest reads certain prescribed prayers, while incense is burned, and the company kneel in couples, each holding a candle. A procession is then formed, the images of Joseph and Mary being carried in front; and the whole company

enter every room in the house, above and below, singing a litany. As the litany ends two or three persons
slip into a room, and shut the door. The rest sing a
carol, in which Joseph begs admittance for himself and
his wife, who can go no farther. To this request a
refusal is given, and the procession goes on until, on
the stroke of midnight, the hostess leads to a room or
attic, or perhaps to the flat roof, where the representa-
tion of a stable has been prepared. There the images of
Joseph and Mary are placed with all possible reverence,
and the ceremony ends. Formerly the procession took
place early on each of the nine evenings; but it came to
be thought irreverent that a religious service should be
sandwiched between games and dances; so now it is
held on one evening only, and shortly before midnight.

This seems the most convenient place in which to
describe a curious old print in the collection of the
Society of Antiquaries (Broadside 305). It was printed
in 1701 by J. Bradford in Little Britain, and sold for
a penny. It measures 10 inches by 8½ inches. It represents the Virgin with the Child in the manger, Joseph
standing by. There are four shepherds, two adoring,
one with a basket, and one with a bagpipe. Three
angels are kneeling, and several are hovering above.
There are sundry beasts and birds around, whose supposed utterances are indicated by Latin labels in their
mouths. The cock crows " *Christus natus est* " (i.e.
Christ is born); the raven croaks " *Quando?*" (when?);
the crow caws " *Hac nocte* " (this night); the ox lows
" *Ubi?*" (where?); the sheep bleats " *Bethlehem* "; and
the angels sing " *Gloria in excelsis* ". In the border are
the instruments of the Passion. A similar idea is

embodied in a quaint little French poem (Macaronic) which tells that of old the animals spoke better Latin than French, and after the conversation above reported adds that the ass brays " *Eamus* " (let us go) and the calf replies " *Volo* " (I am willing).

25. THE CHILDREN'S CHRISTMAS

The mediæval Church did not, on the whole, do its duty by the children. Perhaps it may be pleaded, by way of excuse, that a celibate priesthood could scarcely be expected to understand children. But at least it remembered that Christmas was emphatically the festival of childhood; and possibly with that fact in view it assigned the commemoration of " the Holy Innocents " to the third day after Christmas. A very pretty recognition of the children's interest in the season was continued for a number of years in the thirteenth century, in the church of the Benedictine Nunnery at Godstowe; where on Innocents' Day the public prayers were said by the little girls of the convent school. Archbishop Peckham put an end to this in 1278.

Another custom of similar purport was long and widely prevalent in cathedral and collegiate churches having schools attached. On St. Nicholas's Day, the 6th December, the boys elected one of their number as " bishop ". He was dressed in full canonicals, and during his term of office enjoyed very substantial privileges. In several inventories of Church property we find mention of mitres, copes, and other vestments of the boy-bishop, apparently of as costly material as those worn by the actual dignitaries. He exercised authority over his comrades of the school or choir, to whom he assigned various offices, some of them posing as priests, some as canons, &c. In some places he was escorted to the church, where he presided as bishop during the service; and afterwards went in procession, singing, from door to door, collecting money, " not begging it as alms, but demanding it as the bishop's subsidy ". Early in the thirteenth century the cathedral dignitaries were called on to act in subordinate positions, as taper- and incense-bearers; but this was forbidden in 1263. The boy-bishop and his train actually took part in the Church services, and in December, 1299, they sang vespers before King Edward I. On St. John's Day (27th December) after Complin they were usually entertained at supper by the dean or one of the canons. On Innocents' Day they went in solemn procession, and performed every part of the Church service except actually saying mass. It is alleged that even this exception was not always maintained; but this is very difficult to believe. The performance culminated in the recitation of a sermon by the boy-bishop (it was probably written for him), and in the statutes of St. Paul's School, 1518, all the scholars are enjoined " to hear the child-bishop's sermon on Innocents' Day ". At the end of Complin—the last evening service—he brought his episcopate to a close by pronouncing the Benediction. If the boy happened to die during his term of office, he was buried with the same honours as if he had actually been a bishop; and the tomb of one of these boys is still to be seen in Salisbury Cathedral.

The custom of electing a boy-bishop was observed at St. Paul's, Canterbury, Winchester, Exeter, Salisbury, York, Newcastle, Beverley, Rotherham, Colchester, Eton, Westminster, and Lambeth; and probably in many other places. Hone goes so far as to say " The ceremony of the boy-bishop is supposed to have existed not only in collegiate churches, but in almost every parish ". This seems to be an exaggeration; but it certainly did exist in a number of common grammar-schools, and in several London parishes, notably St. Mary at Hill, St. Andrews Holborn, and St. Nicholas Olaves. There are indications that it was specially favoured where there was a dedication in the name of St. Nicholas, who was deemed the especial patron of schoolboys. It was suppressed in England by proclamation dated 22nd July, 1542; there was a partial revival in Queen Mary's time; but we hear no more of it after her demise. On the Continent it obtained in Switzerland, France, and Spain; but gradually became debased, " irreverent and foolish ", and was finally extinguished at Zug in Switzerland, in 1797. There have, however, been local revivals within the last few years both in England and on the Continent. The plan seems to be that the parish clergyman selects the " bishop " from among the members of a boys guild.

Another curious custom, in recognition of Christmas as peculiarly the children's festival, is that still practised at Rome. The Church of Ara Coeli, which stands above a lofty flight of 124 marble steps, is said to occupy the site, and to be built from the materials, of the ancient temple of Jupiter Capitolinus. It commemorates by its dedication an absurd story of a vision seen ·by Augustus Cæsar of a Crowned Infant seated in a star. In it is preserved an image of the Holy Child, artistically carved in olive wood, crowned and jewelled, and swaddled in gold and silver tissue. This " Bambino " is supposed to have miraculous powers; and it is taken out in its own carriage, attended by its own servants, to visit the sick, who hope for healing through its imaginary virtues. All through the Christmas season it lies in the church crib, and is visited by thousands. On a platform before it little boys and girls of all classes recite little speeches in honour of the Infant Saviour. " They say their pieces " (says Countess Martinengo) " with an infinite charm, that raises half a smile and half a tear." Another writer says: " They have the vivid dramatic gift, the extraordinary absence of self-consciousness that is typical of Italian children; ·and their so-called ' preaching ' is anything but a wooden repetition of a lesson learnt by heart." On the Octave of Epiphany there is a great procession; the Bambino is carried out to the open space at the top of the steps, where " a priest raises it on high, and solemnly blesses the Eternal City ".

26. PURITAN HOSTILITY TO CHRISTMAS

Reference has been made to the Puritan hostility to Christmas. This is much more easily explained than justified. It was not that Puritanism was generally averse to mirth, though there were ascetic Puritans as well as ascetic Papists. After all, there is not very much to choose between the Papists at Coventry, who burned a woman for possessing the scriptures in English, and the Puritan at Banbury, who " hanged his cat on Monday for killing of a mouse on Sunday ". However, the Puritans were so deeply impressed with the sanctity of the Lord's Day that they transferred to it not only all the stringency of the Law of Moses respecting the Sabbath, but much of the spirit of rabbinical tradition. Now the Unreformed Church had quite subordinated the Lord's Day to the great ecclesiastical festivals; and the Anti-puritan party under Elizabeth and James I showed a like inclination. The Puritans thought that festivals of mere human institution, when thus exalted above a Sabbath of divine obligation, became objectionable, and had better not be observed. The first two Stewart kings, on the other hand, sought to extinguish the rather austere Puritan Sabbath by encouraging Sunday games, and to this end put forth the notorious *Book of Sports*. This declaration of war against the Puritan ideal provoked an assault on all those Church festivals which were thus put in open competition with the Sabbath; and as Christmas was the most popular of them all, on it were poured out the vials of the fiercest indignation. Pamphlets were published in which it was denounced as at once heathenish and popish, and its observance was declared to be sinful!

This was in close accord with the sentiment which then prevailed in Scotland. The religious movement in that country had been not merely a Reformation, it was a Revolution. Its leaders, Knox, Melville, and the rest, thought the Romanized Church too bad to be mended; in their view it must be ended, and a new beginning made, strictly on the model which they believed they had found in the New Testament. Now certainly the New Testament makes no mention of ecclesiastical festivals; so the new beginning included the sweeping of them all away, Yule among the rest. On the 26th December, 1583, the Glasgow Kirk Session put five persons to public penance for keeping " the superstitious day called Yule ". Ten years later, in 1593, the same Glasgow session ordained that keepers of this feast should be debarred from the privileges of the Church, and punished by the magistrates; and in 1649 the General Assembly appointed a commission to report on " the druidical customs observed at the fires of Beltane, Midsummer, Hallow-e'en, and Yule "; no doubt with a view to their more effectual suppression. But the end of it was merely that all the worst of the old Christmas customs were transferred to New Year's Day.

In the Scottish Highlands the Presbyterian order and the Puritan sentiment were far less dominant than in the more southern counties, and in them Prelacy and Roman Catholicism each had numerous and influential adherents. In these therefore Christmas persisted in surviving, in spite of Kirk Sessions and General Assemblies. But it would seem from Mrs. Grant's *Popular Superstitions of the Highlands* that down to the latter part of the eighteenth century its observance was more festive than religious, consisting for the most part of games, dancing, feasting, and tippling. Moreover, to the Puritan extremists *any* recognition of Christmas, whether festive or religious, was equally offensive. It was much the same across

the Atlantic. It is said that in one of the New England
settlements a number of young men proposed to celebrate Christmas by a football match; but the governor
intervened, saying, " If their conscience forbids them
to work, my conscience forbids me to allow them to
play ". Some compensation for the suppressed Christmas was found in the newly instituted " Thanksgiving
Day " on the last Thursday in November.

In 1633 William Prynne, a fanatical Puritan lawyer,
published a huge volume more than half as big as the
Bible, to prove the sinfulness of almost every kind of
amusement, but especially of stage plays and Christmas festivities. The title of this amazing monument of
learned folly is *Histriomastix, or the Players' Scourge*.
In it he denounces all Christmas games and feasting
as a wicked survival of the heathen Saturnalia. But
he does not seem seriously averse to a sober religious
recognition of the anniversary. His fanatical hostility
to all sorts of sport and merriment would probably
have been laughed at and forgotten, but for the brutal
punishment inflicted on him for his foolish book. The
effect of setting him in the pillory and cutting off his
ears was to exalt a crank into a hero and a martyr.

Most of the English Puritan leaders had a great
admiration for the Church of Scotland, which they
deemed one of " the best reformed Churches "; and
political exigencies, on the breaking out of the Civil
War, gave an enormous impetus to Scottish ideas in
England. These ideas were acquiesced in, no doubt
in loyalty to the " Solemn League and Covenant ", by
many who regarded them with little sympathy. Perhaps
it was by way of compromise that, in 1642, a volume of

thirty-six metrical psalms appeared, set to secular ballad tunes. The title was " Psalmes or Songs of Sion, turned into the language and set to the tunes of a strange land. By W[illiam] S[latyer], intended for Christmas Carols, &c.". But " The New Forcers of Conscience ", as Milton called them, would have no compromise; and so in 1644, when for a season Puritanism was in power under the Long Parliament, the Monthly Fast was appointed for Christmas Day. It was by this time a somewhat risky business to defend the old order. So in 1645 a satirical tract appeared with the following title: " The Arraignment, Conviction, and Imprisoning of Christmas on St. Thomas day last, and how he broke out of prison in the holidays and got away. . . . With a Hue and Cry after Christmas . . . and what shift he was fain to make to save his life. . . . Printed by Simon Minc'd Pye for Cissely Plum Porridge, and to be sold . . . at the sign of the Pack of Cards in Mustard Alley in Brawn Street."

On 22nd December, 1647, the town crier of Canterbury, by order of the Mayor, proclaimed a market on Christmas Day following. On that day, however, being Saturday, only about a dozen shops were opened. These were stormed by an angry mob, and compelled to close. A few of the rioters were committed to prison, but were forcibly released. The Sunday passed peaceably; but on Monday the rioting was renewed, and several persons were seriously injured. Peace was restored by an agreement between the leaders of the two factions " that no man shall further question or trouble them ". On 24th December, 1652, about four months before Cromwell dispersed it, the Parliament gave order " That no observation shall be had of the five-and-twentieth day of December, commonly called Christmas Day; nor any solemnity used or exercised in churches upon that day in respect thereof ".

But surely the limit was reached in 1656, when a Puritan crank named Hezekiah Woodward printed a tract with this amazing title: " Christmas Day, the old Heathens' Feasting Day in honour to Saturn their Idol-God, the Papists' Massing Day, The Superstitious Man's Idol Day, The Multitude's Idle Day, Satan's That Adversary's Working Day, The true Christian Man's Fasting Day, Taking to heart the Heathenish customs, Popish superstitions, ranting fashions, fearful provocations, horrible abominations committed against the Lord, and His Christ on that day and dayes following." It may suffice to add that the sequel was worthy of the title-page.

In Evelyn's *Diary* we read that on Christmas Day, 1657, he and others were arrested while engaged in worship in Exeter Chapel, and were detained for several hours. However, they were allowed to finish the service, which included a celebration of the Holy Communion.

Indeed there are indications that the Cromwellian regime was less intolerant than that of the Long Parliament; and in spite of restrictions Christmas managed to survive, both in its religious and its festal aspects. This at least may be gathered from the following title-page: " Make roome for Christmas; or Remember your Christmas Box: being a delightful new Book full of merry Jests, rare Inventions, pretty conceits, Christmas Carols, pleasant Tales and witty Verses, written by Lawrence Price, 1657, who wishes well to all those that bear goodwill to Rost Beef, Plum pottage, white loaves, Strong beer, warm Clothes, good fires, and soft Lodgen."

The blunders of well-meaning people are often, in their effect, worse than crimes; and it is fairly open to question whether the beheading of Charles I was in the long run half so harmful to the Puritan interest as the blunder of trying to suppress the Old English Christmas. One thing is certain; when " Old Christmas returned " after the Restoration, it was with a new face. The violent reaction against Puritanism led to the degradation of a great Christian anniversary to a mere heathenish Yule-tide holiday; and instead of the old carols to the praise of the Babe of Bethlehem, the Cavalier rhymesters poured forth rollicking songs to the praise of " Plum pudding, goose, capon, minced pies, and roast beef ".

Meanwhile the misdirected Puritan conscientiousness persisted in some quarters for three or four generations. Far into the eighteenth century grave Presbyterian divines preached against the observance of Christmas; and as late as 1830 hymn-books were in use, in Baptist and other congregations, which either made no provision at all, or barely admitted one or two poor hymns, suitable for a commemoration of the Holy Nativity.   In Scotland the Puritan tradition so far survives that even to this day the recognition of Christmas, either in its religious or its festive aspect, is confined to a minority of the population. In most places business goes on as usual.

27. MUMMING

Let us now turn from the more definitely religious to the purely festive aspect of Christmas and its customs; and first of *Mumming*. The dictionaries define this as " making diversion in disguise "; and the merrymakers who are called Mummers in England were called *Guisards* in Scotland. Throughout the British Isles this was for ages a favourite sport, not at Christmas only, but on other festive occasions. In Ireland it was most prevalent on May Day, and in Scotland about the New Year. But in England Christmas and Easter, especially the former, have been the favourite seasons of the Mummers; the tradition being that both mumming and carol-singing legitimately begin on St. Thomas's Day—the shortest in the year. A familiar old ditty runs thus:

> " To shorten winter's sadness
> See where the nymphs with gladness
> Disguisèd all are coming
> Right wantonly a-mumming,
>   With a fal-lal-la."

It was customary, though not universal, for the girls to dress as boys, and the men as women; and thus disguised to visit the neighbours' houses, singing, dancing, and partaking of good cheer. In many places the performers, if sufficiently skilful, would execute a sword dance. This was altogether different from the Scottish sword dance, and, though usually introduced with some harmless buffoonery, was a really artistic performance; the swords, in the course of the dance, being plaited together in the form of a " rose " or star. As lately as the middle of the nineteenth century it was practised in Durham county, in the Yorkshire dales, and (with some difference) in Devon. It is even continued to this day in the neighbourhood of Flamborough. Elsewhere the Morris dance was affected—though this was usually thought more seasonable at May Day and Whitsuntide—and the hobby-horse was not forgotten.

Where anything beyond dancing was attempted, it usually took the form of a rude burlesque drama, with plenty of fighting. The characters were various, but they generally included a bully, who was killed, and a doctor, by whom he was resuscitated. The leader commonly spoke a ridiculous prologue, varying in different places; one of the drollest, used in Somerset, is as follows:

> " Here comes I, liddle man Jan,
>   With my girt zword in my han';
>   If you doant all dew as you be told by I,
>   I 'll zend ye all to York vor to maake apple pie."

The performance was usually pure buffoonery, but sometimes there was a simple plot, such as the rescue of a Christian maiden from the clutches of a terrible Turk.

In the most widespread of the mummeries the leading characters are St. George, Alexander King of Egypt, Hector—sometimes called Slasher, The Dragon, and Doctor Brown. The prologue is spoken sometimes by Father Christmas, and sometimes by a small boy in a scarlet vest, who personates Robin Redbreast. In the Cornish version St. George kills in succession the Dragon, the Turkish Knight, and the Giant, each of whom is cured by the Doctor. He, after the last cure, is given a basin of " girdy grout ", and is then kicked out; and the epilogue is spoken by Judas with the bag, or by

> " Little Devil Doubt;
> Give him money or he 'll sweep ye all out."

Some have described these Mummery Plays as a degradation or burlesque of the old Miracle Plays; but this is very unlikely. They are more probably a survival from pre-Christian times. There was a custom, in many parts of the Roman Empire, of going about on New Year's Day in masks, often of animal faces, in skins of beasts, and in women's dresses. This practice was strongly condemned by the clergy from the fourth century onward; specimens of their denunciations are extant from at least eight different countries. If we may judge from the analogy of what still goes on in Western Africa, these animal masks were worn for the due performance of sacrificial or magical rites, the wearers being priests or members of secret societies, whom the uninitiated supposed to be demons. This belief would be fostered by the early Christian clergy, to create a greater horror of idolatry. It is almost certain that some such masquerade is the explanation of the Witches' Sabbath on Walpurgis-Nacht.

It being alleged, whether truly or falsely, that crime was facilitated by the disguises, and especially the masks worn by mummers, order is said to have been given by Henry VIII that all mummers wearing visors should be apprehended as vagabonds, and committed to prison for three months, or fined at the king's pleasure.

In some places the Mummery took the form of a Dance of Fools, the dancers wearing motley, with caps and bells. But this belonged less to Christmas than to the New Year and Plough Monday.

In Somerset, and no doubt elsewhere, mumming degenerated into *Mumping*, that is, plain undisguised begging. In many west-country villages the poor old women go around on St. Thomas's Day soliciting seasonable gifts, which it is deemed uncharitable to refuse. In Gloucestershire this is called " Thomasing "; in Warwickshire " Corning "; and in Kent " going a gooding ". A variety of " mumping rhymes " are current in various places, of which one heard in Somerset may serve for a sample:

" Christmas is coming, the beef is getting fat;
Please drop a penny in a poor man's hat!"

Formerly, in return for the expected alms, the mumpers offered sprigs of evergreens, useful for home decoration.

28. HODENING, SCHIMMEL, ETC.

In some parts of Kent, and round about Richmond, in Yorkshire, there was a custom the purely heathen origin of which is obvious. The head of a horse, either a skull or a wooden effigy, was fixed to a pole, and its jaws snapped by means of a string. The party carried handbells and sang songs, for which they expected meat and drink, or money. In Kent the head was made of wood, and its mouth was open for contributions. The ditty was:

> " Three jolly hodening boys
> Lately come from town,
> For apples or for money
> We search the country roun'."

Some of the Kentish wagoners used to keep the head in their stables through the year " for luck ".

A similar practice existed in some parts of Wales. The skull was dressed with ribbons, and carried by a man under a white sheet. The jaws were made to bite anyone it could lay hold of, who was only released on payment of a forfeit. This was called " Mari Llwyd ". E. J. Newell, in his *History of the Diocese of Llandaff*, says that the custom survived at Cardiff as late as 1886, if not later.

It is hard to conceive that Hodening, or Mari Llwyd, could ever have any relation to Christmas. They seem to be either an unintelligent survival, or a designed caricature of some custom of the pre-Christian Yule. The word " hodening " is evidently reminiscent of Odin, who, whatever else he may have been, was certainly a Sky-god. He was represented as a stately man with one eye, there being only one sun in the firmament. He was wrapped in a blue mantle spangled with stars; and rode on a white horse that was swifter than the wind. The horse's head can scarcely be anything else than a relic of Odin's horse Sleipnor.

The German counterpart of this toy is called the " Schimmel "—the Grey or Fusty One. The horse's head is fixed to a pole, and this, sometimes, to a man who goes on all fours, covered with a white cloth.

Elsewhere the horse is formed by three or four lads, one of whom is the rider. He is veiled, and sometimes carries on his head a pot with glowing coals, which shine through openings that represent eyes and mouth. The " Schimmel Reiter " is sometimes accompanied by a " Bear "—a boy dressed in straw, who plays the part of a bear chained to a pole.

In other parts of Germany the head is that of a buck or goat, usually made of wood, with a jaw that clatters. It butts children who cannot say their prayers. This is the " Klapperbock " or " Habergais ".

In Denmark, Norway, and Sweden the " Julebuk ", with a buck's head and dressed in a hide, butted the children whom he met in his peregrinations. Sometimes the name was applied to a straw puppet. There was a story of a girl who danced with a straw Julebuk, and found that her partner was none other than Satan himself. Another Julebuk was carried off by the Evil One whom he had mimicked. A grim story was told in one of the Yorkshire dales (where Scandinavian customs and traditions long survived) of a man who, early in the nineteenth century, went about in a black ox-hide with the horns above his head; he was stabbed to death by the village idiot, who gleefully boasted that he " had killed the devil ".

29. WASSAILING

Somewhat akin to mumming is *wassailing*. " Wassail!" was the old Anglo-Saxon drinking pledge, equivalent to " your health "; to which the response was " Drinkhaile!" At the Saxon Yule feast it was quite

usual, without any feeling of irreverence, to drink
" Wassail to the Lord!" The Wassail Bowl was indispensable at an Old English Christmas feast. At Jesus
College, Oxford, there is a huge silver-gilt bowl, formerly used at such celebrations, which will hold nearly
ten gallons, and the ladle half a pint.

The Wassail Bowl was considered appropriate not
only to Christmas, but also to New Year's Eve and
Twelfth Night. At Court, and no doubt elsewhere, it
was in daily use during all the twelve days of the festive
season, and was brought in with more or less of ceremony. In the Ordinances for the household of King
Henry VII the following occurs with reference to
Twelfth Night: " Item, the chappell to stand on one
side of the Hall" (probably the choristers of the Chapel
Royal), " and when the Steward cometh in at the Hall-
door with the Wassell, he must crie three times ' Wassell, Wassell, Wassell,' and then the chappell to answere
with a good song ". The correct charge of the Wassail
Bowl was " lamb's wool "; a mixture of ale with
roasted apples, sugar, and spice. To this Shakespeare
seems to allude, when he makes Puck say:

> " Sometimes lurk I in a gossip's bowl
> In very likeness of a roasted crab ";

and he describes winter as the season " When roasted
crabs hiss in the bowl ". Herrick bids us:

> " Crown the bowl full
>   With gentle lamb's wool—
> Add nutmeg, sugar, and ginger,
>   With store of ale too;
>   And this ye must do
> To make the wassail a swinger."

Here are two recipes said to have been used in the royal kitchen in 1633. It will be observed that in the first, as in Herrick's rhyme, the apples are not separately mentioned.

(1) Set ale on the fire to warm, boil a quart of cream with two or three whole cloves, add the beaten yolks of three or four eggs, stir all together, and pour into the ale: add sops or sippets of fine Manchet or French bread; put them in a basin, and pour on the warm mixture, with some sugar and thick cream on that; stick it well with blanched almonds, and cast on cinnamon, ginger, and sugar, or wafers and comfits.

(2) Boil three pints of ale; beat six eggs, the whites and yolks together; set both to the fire in a pewter pot; add roasted apples, sugar, beaten nutmegs, cloves, and ginger; and, being well brewed, drink it while hot.

The origin of the name " lamb's wool " is quite unknown. The only etymology we have met with is that suggested by the antiquarian Vallancy. He says that the bowl, with its compound of apples and ale, was common to all great festivals, especially Hallow-e'en, which was dedicated to the angel or spirit who was supposed to keep guard over fruit, seeds, &c. Accordingly that day, in some Celtic dialect, was called " La mas ubhal ", i.e. Apple Day; which by easy corruption became " lamasool ", and finally " lamb's wool ". But why the name of a day should be transferred to that of a beverage is not easy to tell.

Query, if the more general use of distilled spirit in the early part of the eighteenth century did not lead to the frequent substitution of Punch for the time-honoured lamb's wool; a change that has not always promoted an increase of sobriety.

In many places it was customary for young men, and elsewhere for maids, to go from farmhouse to farmhouse with a great wooden bowl of spiced ale, gaily bedecked with ribbons and garlands, inviting the inmates to drink " Wassail " to the season. The custom continued in Gloucestershire far down into the nineteenth century, and perhaps is not yet quite extinct. The song which accompanied the visit was a rollicking Bacchanalian ditty, beginning:

> " Wassail, wassail all over the town!
> Our toast it is white, our ale it is brown,
> Our bowl is made of a maplin tree;
> We be good fellows all—I drink to thee."

Then follow benedictions on the master and mistress, the horse, the ox, and the next year's crop; and the song concludes:

> " Be there here any maids?   I suppose there be some;
> Sure they 'll not let young men stand on the cold stone:
> Sing hey-ho, maids, tirl back the pin,
> And the fairest maid in the house let us all in."

In Herefordshire, on Christmas Eve, the oxen were visited after supper, and a health was drunk in strong ale or cider to the best or favourite ox. A large cake, with a hole in it, was then hung on the ox's horn; he was tickled to make him toss it, and omens were drawn from the way it fell. The usual incantation was to this effect:

> " Here 's to thy pretty face, and thy white horn:
> God send thy master a good crop of corn,

Both wheat, rye, and barley, and all sorts of grain;
Next year, if we live, we 'll drink to thee again."

The party then returned to the house, but found the door fast bolted. It was only opened when someone had guessed what had been provided for supper, or when a merry song had been sung; after that the remainder of the night was passed in feasting and jollity.

Wassailing of trees, in Devon, Somerset, and elsewhere, is something quite different, and belongs to *Old* Christmas Eve, i.e. 5th January. It will be treated of in its proper place.

In Yorkshire the Wassail Bowl has long been obsolete, though the name, in its variant " Wessel-cup " or " Vessel-cup " still survives. But what the children carry about is the Yule Baby, already described. The song that accompanies it, certainly the best of the Wassail songs, begins:

" Here we come a-wassailing
    Among the leaves so green;
Here we come a-wandering
    So fair to be seen:
Love and joy come to you,
    And to you your wassail too;
And God bless you, and send you a Happy New Year."

In the Black Country of Staffordshire a rabble of young urchins make night hideous from St. Thomas's Day to Twelfth Night. They carry neither Wassail Bowl nor Yule Baby; but yell, in every variety of discord,

" A pie sat in a pear tree, the hen sat clucking by;
I wish you a Merry Christmas, and every day a pie;

A pocket full of money, a cellar full of beer,
And a good fat pig in the pig-sty to last you all the year.
The roads are very dirty, my shoes are very thin,
Please, good mistress and master, chuck a penny in.
    A pie, a pie," &c., *ad libitum.*

30. CHRISTMAS EVE

We have already referred to Christmas Eve as the accredited time for placing the seasonable decorations, evergreens, &c., both in house and church. This, though the most obvious, was not the only preparation for the feast which was more or less tinged with superstition. In many places, especially in Scotland, before the Reformation, it was almost a matter of religious obligation to emphasize the holiday aspect of the season. On Christmas Eve the house must be thoroughly cleaned, all borrowed articles returned, all tools laid aside, no lint allowed to remain on rock or wheel; and such work as could not be completed was stopped, and as far as possible made to look as if it were complete. Finally, a cake was baked for every person in the house; and if anyone's cake happened to be broken, it was an omen of ill luck to the person for whom that cake was intended. These cakes were usually flavoured with caraway; and their circular or annular form has been thought to indicate a survival from the heathen sun-worship of Yule-tide.

There are many customs in many countries relating to Christmas cakes, most of which seem to be survivals of old-time superstitions. Not much of this would seem to attach to the Christmas cake of East Yorkshire —just an ordinary " spiced cake ", with raisins, cur-

rants, lemon peel, &c.; or to the " wigs ", or caraway
buns, which in Shropshire were dipped in ale. But
in other places " Yule dows " were given by bakers to
their customers—small images of paste, human or
animal in form. Such are common in many parts of
France and Germany; sometimes the cakes actually
represent the Holy Child; elsewhere they are oblong,
adorned with His figure in sugar. In many places the
cakes are horned, and French ploughmen give to the
poor as many of them as they have oxen or horses. In
some parts of Catholic Germany magical powers
are ascribed to bread baked on Christmas Eve and
moistened with Christmas Dew. This, it is said, will
never grow mouldy, and is a cure for snake bites.
The notion seems to be associated with the antiphon
" Rorate Coeli desuper ", i.e. " Drop down dew, ye
heavens, from above, &c.", which is sung at Vespers
during Advent. A similar superstition is found in
the south of France and in the Italian Tyrol. In
Sweden and Denmark a cake in the form of a boar
stands on the table throughout the festive season,
evidently connected with the cultus of the Boar's Head,
of which we have to treat hereafter.

In Poland monks bring round small wafers of flour
and water, stamped with sacred figures, and blessed
by a priest. Christmas Eve is a strict fast; but when
the first star appears the feasting begins. A few straws
are scattered under the table, and a chair is left vacant
for the Holy Child. All the members of the household,
servants included, break the aforesaid wafers between
them, exchanging mutual good wishes. After supper
the children are led to another room, where Father

Christmas—or as he is called in Poland " The Star
Man "—appears in his proper person. He is often the
parish priest in disguise; he examines them in the
catechism, reproves those who give wrong answers,
and tells the rest that he has brought them rewards
for their good conduct. These are brought in by young
lads, who carry a large illuminated paper star, and sing
carols.

In Roumania the traditional Christmas cakes are thin
dry leaves of dough, eaten with honey, syrup, or other
flavouring.   These are supposed to represent the
swaddling clothes of the Holy Child. In Greece the
Christmas cake has a cross at the top. After supper on
the sacred Eve nothing is removed from the table, in
the hope that Christ will come and eat during the
night. Analogous to this was an old Welsh custom of
unbolting all the outer doors on Christmas Eve, in
case the Holy Family should wish to enter.

Christmas Eve being a fast in Roman Catholic
countries, fish is in great demand. At Hamburg and
other parts of Germany, and in Styria, carp is eaten for
supper; in Saxony and Thuringia, herring salad; in
Brittany, cod; in Italy eels are specially popular. At
Whitstable, in Kent, the fishermen were accustomed to
choose eight of the largest whiting from every boat;
these were sold separately, and their price reserved for
a feast on Christmas Eve in honour of St. Rumbald, the
supposed patron of the fishery. Naturally the eve
came to be called " Rumbald's Night ". A similar
custom is said to have obtained at Folkestone.

Most schoolboys remember the story of a king who
died of indigestion, caused by eating too greedily of

lamprey pie. By ancient custom a lamprey pie is annually presented to the king at Christmas by the city of Gloucester; the custom is sometimes costly, as lampreys are often difficult to procure at that season.

The Gloucester custom reminds us of numerous local traditions relating to Christmas pies. We shall have something to say hereafter on the English mediæval pie. It may suffice here to mention that the more ordinary pie was supposed to occupy the attention of the housewife on Christmas Eve; and that, if we may believe Herrick, the holy season did not always afford it adequate protection from hungry and predaceous members of the professionally unemployed. He bids us

> " Come guard this night the Christmas pie,
>   That the thief, though ne'er so sly,
>   With his flesh-hook don't come nigh
>   To catch it
>   From him who alone sits there
>   With his eye still in his ear,
>   And a deal of nightly fear,
>   To watch it."

In Tyrol, on St. Thomas's Day, an elaborate pie is baked which is marked with the sign of the cross and sprinkled with holy water before it is put in the oven. It is not eaten till St. Stephen's Day or Epiphany, when it is cut by the housefather with considerable ceremony. Each maidservant has also a pie, which she takes home to share with her kinsfolk. If a lover offers to carry her pie, that is understood to be a *proposal*, which she accepts or not according to circumstances.

31. THE YULE LOG

A seasonable Christmas, in England, is a cold one; and our ancestors were much of the opinion of Charles Lamb, that of all the enjoyments of the season the most indispensable is " a large, heaped-up, all-attractive fire ".[1] Our familiar grates for economizing coal are quite a modern invention; the old English Christmas fire blazed upon a wide open hearth, as it still does where wood or peat is the fuel most in vogue. In preparation for the festival a huge log was selected beforehand, as large as the firedogs would conveniently sustain. In some places it was the whole trunk of a tree, which had been selected at Candlemas. In Scotland it was commonly a piece of a birch tree, stripped of its bark and dried beforehand; whence the proverb, used for one who was extremely poor, " He's as bare as a birk on Yule e'en ". The Yule Log[2] was sometimes brought home with considerable ceremony; drawn with ropes by many willing hands, it being thought—or at least said—that all who helped were thereby insured against witchcraft for the ensuing year. Herrick sings:

> " Come, bring with a noise,
> My merry, merry boys,
> The Christmas log to the firing;
> While my good dame, she
> Bids you all be free,
> And drink to your heart's desiring.

[1] The familiar association of Christmas with severe weather is a tradition inherited from the years before the rectification of the Calendar. Christmas, old style, coincides approximately with Epiphany, new style, when the temperature is usually lower than at new style Christmas. Similarly the old May Day corresponds with 13th May of our modern reckoning, when we may generally " go a-maying ", or even sing " Somer is ycomen in " without any serious feeling of incongruity.

[2] In Cornwall it was commonly called " The Mock ".

" With the last year's brand
Light the new block, and
For good success in his spending
On your psalteries play,
That sweet luck may
Come, while the log is a-teending."

In Provence the whole family go out on Christmas
Eve to bring in the log, which should be cut from a fruit
tree. The bearers walk in line, the eldest foremost and
the rest in order of seniority. A carol is sung, praying
for fertility in field and fold, house and vineyard. The
youngest child pours wine on the log " in the name of
the Trinity ", and it is then thrown on the fire. In
France it was sometimes four feet long; it was always
kindled at one end, and replaced on the hearth every
evening until consumed or till Twelfth Night. If any
of it still remained it was carefully preserved as a
charm against lightning, and against chilblains during
that winter. In Normandy, before the Revolution, it
was usual to extinguish the household fire, and kindle
the log with a flame procured from a lamp in the
nearest church. Sometimes, when the log was duly
placed, and before it was kindled, the prettiest girl in
the company was seated on it, and her health drunk
by all present. In other places the children were
warned not to sit on the log lest they should catch the
itch. Another strange custom was to chalk a rude
figure of a man on the log before it was ceremoniously
lighted. One would think this must have been a dim
reminiscence of human sacrifice in heathen times. In
many places the presents for the children were arranged
on the Yule log. Almost everywhere the custom was

that a remnant of the log should be reserved to kindle the new log next Christmas. Sometimes the remnant was kindled afresh on Candlemas Eve, and after blazing awhile was quenched, and preserved as a charm against fire and other misfortunes. Akin to this was a custom in the Netherlands of kindling a splinter of fir wood, quenching it when half-burned, and placing it under the bed as a charm against lightning. In Brittany it is still usual to light the log—always with a brand rescued from last year—at the moment when midnight sounds from the church tower. The very widespread practice of kindling the new log with a remnant of the old seems like the survival of an ancient Celtic notion of a perpetual sacred fire; of which we have more definite illustrations in Ireland.

A very common superstition is that, unless the maids wash their hands before touching the log, the fire will burn dull. In some parts of Yorkshire it was thought that a squinting or barefooted person would bring ill luck, if he came in while the log was burning. Many northern and western customs appear to favour the view that the Yule log is a survival from the Norsemen; among whom, it is said, the Yule fire burned in honour of Thor, and was maintained with logs of his tree, the oak.

The Yule log is an important matter in Dalmatia, Croatia, and Serbia. Not Christmas Eve, but Christmas morning, is the time of its cremation. The tree, or several young trees, are felled before sunrise with some ceremony; corn being thrown on them, with the words " Good morning, Christmas!" As they are carried in, lighted candles are held on each side of the

door; and as the housefather enters with the first log,
corn or wine is thrown on him by one of the family.
Sometimes the girls adorn the log with leaves and
flowers, or with red silk and gilt wire. Sometimes corn
and wine are poured on it, and a plough-share and an
orange set upon it, " that the corn may grow well and
the beasts be healthy ". It is arranged beforehand who,
not of the family, shall first enter the house. He comes
early in the morning, and shakes corn out of his glove
on the threshold, saying, " Christ is born ". One of
the family sprinkles corn upon him, saying, " He is
born indeed ". (These phrases, it scarcely needs to
be said, are the regular Christmas salutation and response.) The visitor then beats the log to make the
sparks fly, and utters a wish for good luck to the household and their farm. Possibly in its origin this ceremonial may have been a solemn rekindling of the
sacred hearthfire, the centre of the family life, and
dwelling-place of the ancestors. It certainly seems
somewhat heathenish.

It must always be remembered that the Yule log,
with all its archaic and sentimental associations, belongs
exclusively to the open hearth. The modern apology,
a billet the size of a quartern loaf, set on the top of a
coal fire in a modern grate, is about as much like
the genuine Yule log as a horse-chestnut is like a
chestnut horse. Still, at Ripon, and probably elsewhere, coopers were wont to dispose of useless knotty
blocks by giving them to customers to serve as Yule
logs. If anything of these was left it was consumed
on old Christmas Eve. Brand, writing in 1777, tells
us that in the north of England a very large block

of coal was often set apart as a substitute for the Yule log.

In Devonshire and Somerset cottages an ashen faggot takes the place of the Yule log. The origin of this was accounted for by a pretty legend. When the shepherds came through the snow to Bethlehem they found the Holy Family suffering from the cold. So the youngest of the shepherds went out and gathered a bundle of ash sticks wherewith to kindle a fire; ash being, it is said, the only wood that will burn freely while green.

Another explanation of the custom relates it to a vague story of King Alfred during his sojourn at Athelney. But considering that the ash was held sacred by the Danes and Norsemen, who were still heathen when the Saxons of Somerset were at least nominally Christian, we are disposed to associate the ashen faggot with the mythic Ash Yggdrasil of the Eddas; by which the world was sustained, the roots of which went down to hell, while its branches soared to heaven. To burn the sacred ash on Christmas Eve might well be a symbolic repudiation of heathenism. As with the Yule log so with the ashen faggot; a remnant should always be reserved to kindle the fire in the following year.

In some places the ashen faggot was associated with a custom which is now, we may hope, generally obsolete. The faggot, of huge size and having nine bands, was kindled on the wide hearth of a farm house, or public house kitchen; the men sat around, and as each band of the faggot gave way, a fresh quart of cider was brought in. If anyone retired, being overcome by the heat, he was expected to pay for another quart of

BRINGING IN THE YULE LOG, PENSHURST PLACE, KENT

After Joseph Nash.

An old-time scene in a great feudal hall showing the ponderous block being hauled into the house with much shouting and laughter.

D 28]

cider by way of penalty. In short, like many other old drinking customs, it was a competition who could imbibe the greatest quantity of liquor without becoming helplessly intoxicated. A less objectionable custom was to associate each of the nine bands with the names of a pair of lovers. The jest was that they whose band was first burnt through would first be married.

If by any chance the Christmas fire should go out, that would be very unlucky; especially when lucifer matches were unknown, and tinder-boxes rather a rarity. For in many places, particularly in the north of England, nobody would oblige another with a kindling at Yule. It was deemed unlucky that any light should leave the house from Christmas Eve till New Year's Day. The fire, therefore, was kept constantly burning, and on this account, at Cleobury Mortimer (Salop) 'the Curfew Bell was not rung during the Christmas season. In some places a bonfire was made in some open space, and kept burning from Christmas Eve till the New Year, so as to be available in case of emergency. In other places, on the contrary, the custom, was *not* to light a fire on Christmas Day *except* with fire borrowed from a neighbour's house. This seems related to the notion of a perpetual sacred fire.

The ashes of the Christmas log were supposed to give fertility to the ground, to rid cattle of vermin, to cure toothache, and to protect the house from fire and ill luck. But to throw them out on Christmas Day would be nothing short of criminal; it would be " throwing ashes in the Saviour's face "!

32. CHRISTMAS CANDLES

In a carol of the earlier half of the nineteenth century we read:

> " Then be ye glad, good people,
> This night of all the year,
> And light ye up your candles;
> His Star is shining near."

Christmas candles can claim a high antiquity. The Jews, at their yearly " Feast of Lights ", in addition to the lamps or candles necessary for illumination, set up many others in honour of the feast; and when our Christian ancestors transferred the name from the feast of Dedication to that of the Nativity, they took over this custom also. It seems to be alluded to by Tertullian, in a passage already quoted, in which he denounces the festal use of lamps as pertaining to heathenism. It was usual all through the Middle Ages to set up on Christmas Eve, both in church and hall, one very large candle in remembrance of the Star of Bethlehem; or perhaps in remembrance of the words of Simeon, who spoke of the Holy Child as " A Light to lighten the Gentiles ". In the buttery of St. John's College, Oxford, there is—or was—a large stone candlestick ornamented with the Holy Lamb, and specially reserved for this purpose. In Scotland, before the Reformation, if the great Christmas candle went out before midnight, it was thought to portend some great calamity to the family. If it continued to burn, then some time after midnight it was extinguished, and the remnant carefully preserved to be used at the " lyke-wake ", i.e. death-watch—of the head of the family.

In Ireland the Yule log is little regarded; but the Christmas candle is of great importance. It is of large size—sufficient to serve for New Year's Eve and Twelfth Night. If there is not a candlestick big enough to receive it, some homely substitute is contrived—perhaps fashioned out of a large turnip. Before lighting, it is decked with holly, or with coloured paper cut in fantastic patterns. A similar custom is said to exist in Finland, and in some parts of Germany.

Early in the last century it was customary in Lancashire villages for the children, on the day before the holidays, each to bring a candle to the schoolmaster. And within living memory grocers and chandlers used regularly to give large Christmas candles to their customers or their children; a fashion which only died out as " dips " and " moulds " gave place to improved methods of illumination. In a colliery village near Oswestry (Salop), early in the last century, it was customary in the evenings of Christmas week to carry about the street boards covered with clay, in which were stuck lighted candles. This custom was confined to the colliers; its origin and meaning seem to be quite forgotten.

In Norway it was usual on Christmas Eve to arrange all the silver and polished pewter in the house so that the light of the Christmas candles should shine on it, as if in benediction. In West Jutland *two* large candles were lighted, to represent the householder and his wife; whichever of them burnt the longer, it was supposed that its representative would outlive the other. Usually in all the Scandinavian countries the Yule candle had to burn all through the night, until the sun arose: it should then be extinguished by the father or the oldest member of the household. The remainder of the candle was smeared on the plough, or used to make the sign of the cross on the cattle, or given to the poultry, or in some other way used as a charm against ill luck.

33. THE CHRISTMAS FEAST

Let us now suppose that we have hung up the holly and ivy, not forgetting the mistletoe; we have listened to the waits and the carol singers, laughed at the mummers, and paid the usual toll to the Wassail Bowl. We have lent a hand toward bringing home the Yule log, eaten our carp or herring salad, laid up all needful provision in our own modest larder, and duly responded to the call of the Christmas bells. And now, it may be, we are accepting an invitation to dine at the Great House of the village. Abraham Lincoln is reported to have said that " he thought the Creator had rather a liking for the Common People, He made so many of them ". But the creators of Christmas literature seem in general to be otherwise minded; for in almost every literary or poetic description of a Christmas feast from an earlier pen than that of Dickens, it is the feast of the Palace, the Castle, or at least the Manor House—where the squire and his worthy dame keep open house throughout the festive season. No doubt here, as elsewhere " distance lends enchantment to the view ". Indisputably the " good old times " as pictured for us by Herrick and Wither, Walter Scott and Washington Irving, have a sort of glamour which makes us wish they could be recalled; but if we were able to do so it is likely we should find the price more than we were willing to pay. Sir Roger de Coverley and Lady Bountiful were excellent people in their way; " take them for all in all we shall not look upon their like again ". But they believed with all the assurance of religious conviction in the divine right of the landlord " to determine who should be associated with him in the cultivation of the soil "; and if, in those good old days, tenant or labourer had so much as dreamed of thinking for himself, or voting against the squire, or saying his prayers otherwise than according to the Act of Uniformity, the very least he could have looked for would have been to be set down for a Puritan, who could have no possible interest in Christmas or any of its festivities.

The ideal English Christmas, to which the fancy of later generations looked longingly backward, was that of Queen Bess or James I, before Puritanism had grown strong enough to be troublesome. To such a Christmas feast let us transport ourselves in imagination. The hall is decked with holly, picturesquely stuck among the antlers and old armour that are its usual adornments. The remains of the Yule log are still discernible on the hearth; the guests are seated at the long tables, with strict regard to social rank. A sound of music is heard outside, the jester gambols in with some extravagant antic, and all the company rise in honour of *The Boar's Head*, carried by the chief cook on a silver dish, wreathed with bay, having in its mouth a lemon or a roasted pippin, and in its ears sprigs of rosemary. It is closely followed by the minstrels, and as many of the upper servants as can be mustered, carrying the subsidiary dishes, and the procession moves slowly up to the high table, singing the never-to-be-forgotten carol:

> " The Boar's Head in hand bear I,
> Bedecked with bays and rosemary;
> And I pray you, my masters, be merry,
> *Quot estis in convivio.*

> " The Boar's Head, as I understand,
> Is the chief service in this land;
> Which thus bedecked with a gay garland,
> *Servite cum cantico.*

> " Our steward hath ordainèd this
> In honour of the King of Bliss,
> Who this day to be served is.
> *In Reginensi Atrio.*

> *Caput apri defero,*
> *Reddens laudes Domino.*[1]

The ceremonial bringing in of the Boar's Head, with music, is a custom of great antiquity. It is distinctly recorded as having been performed " according to the manner " at a royal banquet in 1170. Of its meaning something will be said hereafter. As to the subordinate dishes, here is a rhyming list from a MS. of the fifteenth century. If of no other interest, it tells

---

[1] This is the form in which the carol has been regularly sung at Oxford for the last two hundred years. The older recension, printed by Wynken de Worde in 1521, gives the third verse as follows:

> " Be glad, lords, both more or less,
> For this hath ordained our steward
> To cheer you all this Christmass,
> The Boar's Head with mustard."

There are several other Boar's Head songs, ranging from the sixteenth to the eighteenth century; but they are of little interest. The older ones are mere doggerel; and the later ones, with allusions to Ceres and Bacchus, Meleager, the Calydonian Boar &c., have nothing in common with genuine folk-song; they are simply academical jokes.

us what in those days was accounted good eating:

> " Then comes the second course with great pride;
> The cranes, the herons, the bitterns by their side,
> The partridge, the plover, the woodcock, and the snipe;
> Larks in hot ' schow '[1] for the ladies to ' pyke ';
> Furmety for pottage and venison fine;
> Umbles of the doe, and all that ever comes in;
> Capons well baked, and knuckles of the roe,
> Raisins, and currants, and other spices mo';
> Good drink also, luscious and fine,
> Blood of Allemaine, Romnay, and wine."

Swan was a standard dish in great houses at Christmastide; according to the Duke of Northumberland's *Household Book*, 1512, five swans were dished for Christmas Day, three for New Year's Day, and four for Twelfth Day. A peacock was a favourite Christmas dish of old time—skinned before roasting, reclothed with his own feathers, and the beak either gilded or holding a sponge saturated with blazing spirit. The custom was that the peacock should be brought in, not by a servant, but by the most distinguished lady of the company. He was, confessedly, dry meat, and was served with abundance of gravy; though we venture to doubt the story of three fat wethers being needed to make gravy for one peacock. Turkey first appears as Christmas fare in 1524. Bustard continued to figure in Christmas menus till the end of the eighteenth century; but the bird has since become practically extinct in England.

Profusion, rather than refinement, was characteristic of those old Christmas feasts. In 1248, when King Henry III was keeping his Christmas at Winchester, he

[1] ? sauce

ordered his treasurer to fill Westminster Hall with poor
people, and feast them for a whole week. Richard II
was even more prodigal in his Christmas feasting.
When Westminster Hall was enlarged and embellished,
he provided 28 oxen, 300 sheep, and game and fowls
without number; feeding 10,000 guests during several
days. One old writer, John of Salisbury, tells of a
Christmas feast that began at 3 o'clock in the afternoon, and ended at midnight; when delicacies were
brought from such remote places as Constantinople,
Syria, Egypt, and Babylon. Here is a bill of fare about
the year 1560 or 1570, including sixteen principal
dishes; (1) a shield of brawn with mustard; (2) a
boiled capon; (3) a boiled piece of beef; (4) a chine of
beef, roasted; (5) a neat's tongue, roasted; (6) a pig,
roasted; (7) chewets,[1] baked; (8) a goose, roasted; (9)
a swan, roasted; (10) a turkey, roasted; (11) a haunch
of venison, roasted; (12) a pasty of venison; (13) a
kid with a pudding in the belly; (14) an olive pye;
(15) a couple of capons; (16) a custard or dowset.
Sixteen other dishes were made up of salads, fricassees,
devised paste, and sundries.

" The Roast Beef of Old England " has been for
ages the *great* Christmas fare. The legend of " Sir
Loin " knighted by Charles II is no doubt apocryphal,
though the table on which the ceremony is said to
have been performed still exists in several places to
vouch for it. But a baron of beef, i.e. two sirloins, not
cut asunder, but joined by the end of the backbone,
is still roasted for the king's table every Christmas Day.

As to what may be called the accessories of the old-

[1] Probably a kind of savoury mince-pie.

time Christmas feast; bread, of course, goes without saying, and there must have been some provision of roots and pot herbs, as beet, carrots, coleworts, parsnips, salsafy, skirrets, and turnips. Potatoes were only introduced in 1586, and were a rarity till after the Restoration. The " furmety " or frumenty of the old rhyming bill of fare (p. 119), according to the oldest formula now extant, was wheat boiled till the grains burst, and when cool strained and boiled again with broth or milk and yolks of eggs. This was the legitimate accompaniment of fat venison or fresh mutton.

In more recent times frumenty was a mawkish concoction of stewed wheat, boiled up with milk, raisins, sugar, and spices. It was lately, and perhaps still is, the regulation Christmas Eve supper in many rural parts of Yorkshire. Elsewhere it was the first thing taken on Christmas morning; ale posset being the last thing drunk on Christmas Eve. In Shropshire the custom was that every farmer should set aside a sack of wheat for the poor; from which on St. Thomas's Day his wife or daughter doled out a pint or a quart to each comer, according to their poverty and the size of their family. This was to make frumenty for the Christmas feast. The custom survived here and there till about 1870; but generally before that time the farmers gave money to the parson instead, to provide clothing for the poor. The aforesaid frumenty was probably an early stage in the evolution of what afterwards became plum porridge; and this in turn, about 1670 or a little earlier, stiffened into plum pudding. That plum porridge was indeed fearfully and wonderfully made. One of its simpler forms was beef or

mutton broth, thickened with brown bread; half-boiled
raisins, currants, prunes, mace, and gingerbread were
added; and when thoroughly done the mixture was
served in a semi-liquid state. Another recipe is to boil
beef and veal with sack, old hock, and sherry, lemon
and orange juice, double-refined sugar, raisins, currants,
and prunes; add cochineal, nutmeg, cinnamon, and
cloves; the whole to be thickened with brown bread and
served in a tureen. This delectable mess was served at
St. James's Palace as late as 1806, possibly later. Sir
Roger de Coverley is made to say (*Spectator*, No. 269)
that he had hopes of a " rigid dissenter " when he saw
him enjoying his plum porridge. In these various
recipes prunes, i.e. plums, form an essential part.
Gradually they seem to have been supplanted by raisins,
&c., so that a plum pudding may be defined as a pudding without plums—*lucus a non lucendo*. A more
serious misnomer is current in rural parts of Somerset;
where raisins are commonly called figs (a real fig is a
" doat-fig "), and our customary Christmas treat is
" figgy pudding ".

But what of the Christmas pie? That was also a
marvellous concoction, in the true etymological sense
of the word. Here is a recipe—wording modernized—
from a MS. written in 1394. " Take a Pheasant, a Hare,
a Capon, two Partridges, two pigeons, and two Conies;
chop them up, take out as many bones as you can, and
add the livers and hearts, two kidneys of sheep, force-
meat made into balls with eggs, pickled mushrooms,
salt, pepper, spice, and vinegar. Boil the bones in a
pot to make good broth; put the meat into a crust of
good paste ' made craftily into the likeness of a bird's

body '; pour in the liquor, close it up, and bake it well; ' and so serve it forth, with the head of one of the birds at one end and a great tail at the other, and divers of his long feathers set cunningly all about him '."

The Christmas pie of Herrick's time was filled with neats' tongues, chicken, eggs, raisins, orange and lemon peel, sugar, and various spices. It is not difficult to imagine the stages of evolution, or devolution, by which this eventuated in our modern mince pie. And in like manner we may well believe that the same ancestry, with somewhat different environment, gave birth to the renowned squab pie of Cornwall. But we must pause here; else we shall be led on to treat of mackerel pie, maggoty pie, and so many others that they say " the devil dares not show himself in Cornwall, lest he should be baked in a pie ".

In Hone's *Table Book*, vol. II, p. 506, the following is quoted from the *Newcastle Chronicle* of 6th January, 1770: " Monday last was brought from Howick to Berwick, to be shipp'd for London, for Sir Hen. Grey, Bt., a pie the contents whereof were as follows, viz., 2 bushels of flour, 20 lbs. of butter, 4 geese, 2 turkeys, 2 rabbits, 4 wild ducks, 2 woodcocks, 6 snipes, and 4 partridges, 2 neats' tongues, 2 curlews, 7 blackbirds, and 6 pigeons. It was made by Mrs. Dorothy Patterson, housekeeper at Howick. It was near nine feet in circumference at bottom, weighs about twelve stones, will take two men to present it to table. It is neatly fitted with a case and four small wheels."

This may serve for the Christmas feast of what people will persist in calling " the good old times "—-

the times of semi-starvation for the many and of riotous luxury for the few. We appreciate them most highly as we look backward through the mist of ages, and fancy ourselves at the festive board—of course " above the salt "—while the minstrels played and sang, and the jesters cracked their smartest jokes, and perhaps the celebrated " Dance of Fools " was performed. The reckless profusion had one redeeming feature; there would be an enormous overplus of broken meat, which on the following day would be distributed among the poor. In this sense it was quite a pardonable exaggeration to say:

> " A Christmas gambol oft could cheer
> The poor man's heart for half the year."

It may be remarked that *sometimes* these old Christmas feasts borrowed the one commendable element of the older Roman Saturnalia, and set forth for once in the year the Brotherhood of Humanity. It was not merely that

> " The heir, with roses in his shoes,
> That night might village partner choose."

It was not unusual for country squires of the better class to keep open house for all comers during Christmas time, " when minstrels and dancers flocked to the hall, and crowds enjoyed right good fare ". We read of one, John Carminow, in Cornwall, who used to do this during the whole twelve days of the feast; providing for his guests 12 fat bullocks, 36 sheep, 20 Cornish bushels of wheat, with hogs, lambs, and fowls of all sorts. Still better, at Penshurst, the home of the

Sidneys, in Queen Elizabeth's time, the distinctions
of rank and fortune were provisionally laid aside; rich
and poor equally shared the squire's bounty; no great
salt-cellar divided the noble from the ignoble guests,
and the dishes did not grow coarser as they receded
from the high table. No wonder that in such cases
the Christmas feast became a bond of union between
all classes, and begat friendly relations between lord
and peasant, which were not easily disturbed. It was
well, surely, that not only from the pulpit but also
from the festal board this gospel should be annually
proclaimed, that He whose birthday was kept with joy
and hallowed mirth was born to be not only " King of
kings and Lord of lords ", but, as St. Francis had
taught long before, to be " Little Brother of all Mankind ".

During the latter half of the eighteenth century the
increasing prosperity of the nation, and improved means
of conveyance, led to a great increase of travelling,
especially among the wealthier classes. A natural result
was a great increase and general improvement of inns,
which at festive seasons like Christmas made ample
provision for expected guests. Hone (*Table Book*, II,
43) gives the Christmas Bill of Fare of the " Bush "
Inn at Bristol for the year 1800. It numbered 150
items, including, besides beef, mutton, lamb, veal,
pork, and venison in every conceivable variety, hares,
rabbits, 39 sorts of birds, 16 sorts of fish, 3 of shell-
fish, 10 kinds of soup—including turtle, boar's head,
pies of various kinds, mince pies, jellies, &c.; but,
strange to say, there is no mention of plum porridge
or plum pudding.

What has here been said about feasting has, no doubt, a distinct reference to the old English Christmas. But wherever, throughout the world, the festival of the Nativity is observed, feasting has a conspicuous place in the programme; and often, as is surely fitting, the feasting gives occasion for generous hospitality. In Serbia, for example, it has long been the custom for every well-to-do family to keep open house for three days; and all comers—friend or enemy, stranger or beggar—are welcome to a place at the table.

34. THE BOAR'S HEAD

We must revert for a moment to the " Song of the Boar's Head ", already quoted. We have called it a carol, and such it is in the strictest sense of the word. It is moreover the oldest *printed* carol in existence, having been printed by Wynkin de Worde in 1521. Various are the explanations that have been given of the prominence of the boar's head at the Christmas feast; and all, except those which are manifestly mere jokes, are more or less of a religious character. According to the law of Moses the swine was an unclean beast; and from the time of the Maccabees or earlier the eating of swine's flesh by a Jew was deemed a formal act of apostasy. It has therefore been suggested that its introduction at the Christmas board was a trophy of emancipation from the old law; Christ having made all meats clean, so that on His birthday Christians might freely eat that which was forbidden to the fathers.

Others say that we have here a survival from the

old Norse folklore. The Boar Saehrimmer furnished the daily meal of the heroes in Walhalla, and on earth his kindred furnished the staple of a feast in honour of Odin. His counterpart may be found in the everlasting pig of the pagan Irish paradise, who furnished the immortal food of the gods.

Not only among the Jews, but also among the Egyptians, and all the Semitic peoples except the Babylonians, swine were held in abhorrence. The same is true of the Cretans, Arcadians, Galatians, and several other of the Celtic tribes, as also of the worshippers of Tammuz (or Adonis) everywhere, who according to the legend was killed by the tusk of a wild boar. By the Irish and Welsh, on the other hand, swine were highly esteemed, pork being generally preferred to beef and mutton. Irish legends tell of monstrous swine being eaten at solemn feasts; and the strange wild story of " The Hunting of Twrch Trwyth " in the *Mabinogion* represents the ancestor or patriarch of all the pigs as coming to Wales from the country of the gods. Yet there seems to have been some tradition of evil associated with them; for until quite recent times, in several parts of Wales, a familiar name for the devil was " The Crop-tailed Black Sow ", *Yr hwch ddu gwta*.

There are numerous pig customs in various parts of Europe to which no religious significance can be attached, but which are still associated with the season of Christmas. In Germany a pig killed shortly before Christmas is partaken of on Christmas Day. Pig's head is one of the chief items at the Christmas Eve supper in Sweden and Denmark. Pig is the principal

Christmas dish in Roumania and Serbia; and in Russia pig's trotters were eaten at the New Year. These practices seem to be survivals from the Yule-tide feasting of prehistoric times, when " the Continental Celts were the pig-breeders and pork-curers of ancient Europe, and supplied Rome and the rest of Italy with bacon ". There may be some connection between them and the fact that in heathen times a hog was the usual sacrifice to Frey. In Sweden a favourite Christmas frolic was to represent this sacrifice in pantomime; the actors being disguised and their faces blackened, and the victim being dressed in a skin and holding a wisp of straw to represent the pig's bristles. The performance was accompanied with music and feats of agility. But none of these customs throws any light on the prominence given to the boar's head in the English Christmas feast.

In the story of Sintram the berserkers are represented as making vows on the boar's head. And although the whole story is pure romance—laid in an age when Christianity was still contending with the remains of northern paganism—it is difficult to think that Fouqué had not some tradition or legend on which to base the incident, and if so it might well be that the bringing of the head to table on Christmas Day was a symbolic renunciation of heathenism; men ate that by which their ancestors had sworn.

But perhaps the best explanation is furnished by the mediæval interpretation of the 80th Psalm; where Satan is " the wild boar out of the wood " who has long wasted the vineyard of the Lord. Now his head is carried in triumph as a testimony of his final defeat by the newborn King; and the bearers chant, in a solemnly festive strain:

> " *Caput apri defero,*
> *Reddens laudes Domino*;"

that is

> " I bear the boar's head,
> Rendering praises to the Lord."

The old solemnity of the boar's head is still regularly observed at Queen's College, Oxford; and it was several times presented at the royal table during the reign of Queen Victoria. The Oxford ceremony is thus described in Husk's *Songs of the Nativity*: " The head, the finest and largest that can be procured, is decorated with garlands, bays, and rosemary; it is borne into the hall on the shoulders of two of the chief servants of the college, and followed by members of the college and the college choir. The carol is sung by a member, usually a fellow, of the college, and the chorus by the choir, as the procession advances to the High Table; on reaching which the boar's head is placed before the Provost, who sends slices of it to those who are with him at the high table; and the head is then sent round to the other tables in the hall, and partaken of by the occupants."

At Hornchurch, in Essex, which is ecclesiastically related to New College, Oxford, the lessee of the tithes was accustomed yearly on Christmas Day to provide a boar's head, dressed and garnished. In the afternoon it was carried to a field adjoining the churchyard, where it became the prize of a wrestling-match. The winner carried it off to a public house, where he and his friends feasted on it with all seasonable merriment. Hone, writing in 1827, says this custom had lasted from time immemorial.

35. CHRISTMAS SPORTS

After the feast come the sports. The Hornchurch wrestling has already been mentioned. As a rule we do not find much attention paid at Christmas to those " manly exercises " which were strenuously cultivated at other seasons, such as shooting, leaping, and the like; nor even to those which might be thought specially seasonable, as curling or skating. The one exception is football. In many parts of Wales great football matches were played on Christmas Day. After morning service the whole population, male and female, of two adjacent parishes would turn out for a game, the goals lying well within each parish; and the game was played with such vigour that it sometimes degenerated into a fight. It seems possible that these matches were originally contests between two clans, or between parties with different racial conditions. In Shetland the men were accustomed to spend the greatest part of the short winter's day in football, not only on the actual feast day, but throughout the whole twelve days of " the yules "; while the evenings were devoted to dancing.

There is one kind of Christmas " sport " which has been customary in many places, which can only be excused on the ground that it is the outcome of some old-time superstition—probably a survival of some forgotten rite of heathen religion. This is the hunting of

certain small creatures; in Suffolk squirrels and owls, and
in many places wrens. Why squirrels and owls should
be persecuted it is hard to say; but there are indications
in folklore that a sacred character was once ascribed to
the wren. Moreover, in several heathen religions we
meet with the killing and (apparently) sacramental eating of sacred animals, in which some mysterious energy
was supposed to be incarnated. We can well understand that a creature treated as sacred in heathen times
would, when heathenism was discredited, be regarded
with disfavour. Now it is said that the Druids took
auguries from the varying note of the wren; wherefore
in Derbyshire it was called " the Devil's bird "; and
yet it was deemed unlucky to kill it. The one-time
sacred character of the little bird seems to explain the
nursery jingle, " Tommy Tit and Jenny Wren are God
Almighty's cock and hen ".[1] It appears that in many
places the rustics did not distinguish between the two;
or rather imagined that the Tit was the male and the
Wren the female. This blunder may seem less astonish-
ing if it be remembered that so educated a man as
Oliver Goldsmith included the mole among animals
of the rat kind; called tortoises and turtles crustaceous
fishes; and made the porcupine a kind of superior
hedgehog!

The original significance of the practice being forgotten, hunting the wren was usually accounted for by
some ridiculous story. In the Isle of Man the story

---

[1] In several counties Cock Robin is substituted for Tom Tit in the nursery jingle. This
naturally suggests the beautiful dirge in Webster's tragedy:

" Call for the Robin Redbreast and the Wren,
Since over shady groves they hover,
And with leaves and flowers do cover
The friendless bodies of unburied men."

was that a malignant fairy or siren, assuming the shape of a beautiful woman, had lured many men to destruction; but at length she was so closely pursued by an avenging knight that she only escaped by taking the form of a wren; in which disguise she is hunted year after year. The dead wren was sometimes kept as a charm against shipwreck: at other times it was the subject of a mock funeral after Midnight Mass. But some of the ditties associated with the custom imply that the bird was formerly eaten. In Ireland the hunting was on St. Stephen's Day—the day after Christmas: the story was that St. Stephen, hiding in a furze bush, was betrayed to his enemies by a wren; so a customary ditty began " The wren, the king of all the birds,[1] was caught on St. Stephen's day in the furze ". Another story was that during a rebellion in the north of Ireland a party of English were asleep, and would surely have been slaughtered by Irish Papists, but were awakened by the noise of wrens dancing and pecking on a drum— for which they were denounced as " the devil's birds ". Whatever the origin of the custom, the little bird was hunted, and when killed was hung in a bush of holly, and carried about by " Wren Boys " or " Droluns ", who called at each house to levy contributions of money or drink. If these were refused, the Wren Boys indicated their displeasure by " rough music ". A similar custom of hunting wrens formerly obtained in some parts of France.

Usually, however, Christmas was the season for good, honest play. It was the feast of the Holy Child, and grave and reverend seniors made themselves chil-

[1] Probably the Golden-crested Wren (*Regulus Cristatus*) is intended.

dren for the time. There would be dancing, of course; never was there a genuine English merry-making without dancing, till pragmatical Prynne discovered that the lads and lasses who footed it to Sellinger's Round were art and part with the daughter of Herodias, when she danced off John the Baptist's head. Then we read of blindman's buff, hot cockles, hunt the slipper, bob-apple, forfeits, shoeing the wild mare, and fox i' th' hole. Shuffle-board, and games with cards and dice were popular. A statute of Henry VII forbade apprentices to play at cards, except during the Christmas holidays: and many who would not participate in games of chance at any other time made an exception in favour of Christmas.

William Lovel, Lord Morley, died in July, 1475. Nine years later Margery Paston sent to inquire how his household kept the Christmas immediately following his death. His widow replied that " there were none disguisings, nor harping, nor luting, nor singing, nor none loud disports; but playing at the tables, and chess, and cards; such disports she gave her folk leave to play, and none other " (see *Paston Letters*, No. 441).

One favourite sport of considerable antiquity, but specially associated with Christmas Eve, is snap-dragon. A quantity of raisins, or other dried fruit, is placed on a broad, shallow dish, brandy is poured over it, and set on fire. The company in turn snatch the fruit out of the blaze, to do which without being scorched needs some dexterity. It is usual to extinguish all the lights in the room while the game is in progress.

36. MASKING

Among the upper classes it was not unusual at
Christmas time to present a *masque*, in which persons
of the highest distinction did not disdain to take a
part. This appears to have been a new fashion introduced in the time of Henry VIII, and to have reached
its highest development under James I. A large number
of Court masques were written by Ben Jonson, who
on the mechanical and scenic side was ably assisted by
the royal architect, Inigo Jones. One of the most notable of these was *The Masque of Christmas*, in which
there were twelve principal and thirteen or fourteen
subordinate characters. " First came *Father Christmas*
with two or three of his guard, and a drum beaten
before him. He wore a close doublet, round hose, long
stockings cross-gartered, white shoes, a high-crowned
hat with a brooch, and a little ruff; he had a long thin
beard, and carried a truncheon. Then came his ten
children, led in a string by Cupid, and each with a
suitable attendant. *Misrule* wore a velvet cap with a
sprig, a short cloak, and a great yellow ruff: his torch-
bearer carried a basket with a cheese and a rope. *Carol*
had a red cap and a long tawny coat, with a flute hanging at his girdle: his torch-bearer carried a song-book,
open. *Minced Pie* was neatly dressed as the cook's
wife: her man carried a pie on a dish, and a spoon.
Gambol appeared as a tumbler, with a hoop and bells:
his torch-bearer was armed with a ' cole-staff '[1] and a
blinding cloth. *Post and Pair*[2] had a pair-royal of aces

---

[1] A staff on which to carry a cole or cowl, i.e. a tub with ears, to be carried on a staff
between two persons.

[2] This was a card game resembling, if not identical with, what is now known as " Poker ".

in his hat; his garment was done over with ' pairs and purs ': his squire carried a box with cards and counters. *New Year's Gift* was like a serving-man, in a blue coat, with an orange, and a sprig of rosemary gilt on his head; his hat is stuck full of brooches, and his collar is made of gingerbread: his torch-bearer carries a ' marchpane ' and a bottle of wine on each arm. *Mumming* wears a pied suit with a visor: his torch-bearer carries a box, and rings it. *Wassail* is a neatly dressed maiden: her page bears a brown bowl, dressed with ribbons and rosemary, before her. *Offering* wears a short gown and carries a porter's staff: his torch-bearer goes before him with a basin and a wyth. Finally, *Baby-cock* is dressed like a little boy, in a fine long coat and a cap with ear-pieces, with bib, muckender, and a little dagger: his usher carries a great cake with a bean and a pease." With all due respect to the undoubted genius of " Royal Ben ", it must be owned that the speeches assigned to these characters are not worthy of his reputation; and the action, apart from the dancing, is mere buffoonery.

It has been thought that mumming was a mere degraded survival of masking; but it would rather seem from this description that masking is a later development and glorification of mumming.

37. THE LORD OF MISRULE

Stow, the antiquarian (died, 1605), tells us that " Anciently there was in the king's house, wherever he lodged, at the Feast of Christmas, a ' Lord of Misrule, or Master of Merry Disport '; and the like also was there in the house of every nobleman of honour or good worship, whether temporal or spiritual. Among them the Lord Mayor and Sheriffs of London had their several Lords of Misrule, ever contending, without quarrel or offence, who should make the most pastime to divert the beholder. These lords began their rule, or rather misrule, on All-Hallows Eve, and continued the same until Candlemas Day; in which space there were fine and subtile disguisings, masks, and mummeries, with playing of cards for counters, nails, and points, in every house, more for pastime than for gain."

The date named seems to give countenance to a conjecture that the " Lord of Misrule " was in some way an impersonation of the malignant power that was supposed to rule, or misrule, the " inverted year ", the season of storms, and frozen streams, and leafless trees; not, of course, the actual devil, but the spirit of winter, the blind god Hoeder, the touch of whose spear had slain " Balder the beautiful, god of the summer sun ". This, it may be said, is somewhat farfetched; but it is certain that in those districts where the population contains a large Scandinavian element the Yule-tide merry-makings had a good deal of heathenism in them. In the north of Yorkshire, for example, it was usual in the early part of the seventeenth century to dance in church after prayers on Christmas Day, and throughout the holiday. A little earlier, in Queen Elizabeth's time, the Lord of Misrule and his crew are said sometimes to have invaded the the church, and thrown the service into confusion. In 1576 Archbishop Grindal issued certain " Articles of

CHRISTMAS REVELS: HADDON HALL, DERBYSHIRE

After Joseph Nash.

A scene in one of the Tudor mansions, which were well suited to the hospitable requirements of the time. The hall rang with the laughter and shouts of relations, friends, and retainers all bent on " keeping their Christmas holiday ".

Inquiry " applicable to the whole Province of Canterbury. One of them was " Whether the minister and churchwardens have suffered any lords of Misrule . . . or any disguised persons or others in Christmas or at May-games, or any morris-dancers . . . to come unreverently into the church or churchyard, and there to dance, or play any unseemly parts, with scoffs, jests, wanton gestures, or ribald talk, namely in the time of Common Prayer ". Nine years later the Puritan John Stubbs wrote, in *The Anatomie of Abuses*, as follows: " The wilde heades of the parish, flocking together, chuse them a graund captaine of mischief, whom they innoble with the title of My Lord of Misrule. Then marche these heathen compaine towards the church and churchyard, their pipers pypyng, drummers thonderyng, their stumpes dauncing, their belles jyngling, their handkerchefes swyngyng about their heads like madmen, their hobbie-horses and other monsters skyrmishing amongst the throng; and in this sorte they go to the churche (though the minister be at praier or preachyng) dauncing and swyngyng their handkerchiefs over their heads in the church, like devilles incarnate, with such a confused noise that no man can heare his owne voyce. Then the foolish people, they looke, they stare, they laugh, they fleere, and mount upon the formes and pewes to see these goodly pageants solemnized in this sort."

It seems convenient to mention, in connection with these disorders, a Yorkshire custom of shouting " Yule!" at the end of the Christmas morning service. This may explain the origin of a nonsense rhyme which can be traced back for several centuries, but to which no rational meaning has ever been assigned:

> " Yule, Yule, Yule,
> Three puddings in a pule,
> Crack nuts and cry Yule!"

In some towns and villages a master of the revels appears to have been publicly appointed to organize the parish festivities. In great houses where a professional jester was kept, the business was usually assigned to him. In the colleges at Oxford (perhaps also at Cambridge) the fellows appointed a member of the college, usually a M.A., to regulate the proceedings of the Twelve Days. In the Inns of Court his function seems to have been rather to stimulate than to regulate. He was called by various names; at Merton College, Oxford, he was " King of Christmas "; at Trinity he was " Emperor "; in many places he was " The Christmas Prince "; but more commonly " The Lord of Misrule ", and in Scotland " Abbot of Unreason ". He was somewhat analogous to the mock king of the Roman Saturnalia; his function being to organize the sports and keep up a continuous round of merriment at least from Christmas Eve to Twelfth Night. He maintained a mock court, and assigned to each one an active share in the business of merry-making. In a great house, or at court, he was well paid for his pains. On one occasion Henry VIII paid £15, 6s. 8d. to his Lord of Misrule; equal to at least £200 of our present currency. At other times wealthy men seem to have assumed the function at their own cost, for the entertainment of the guild, society, or town in which they were specially interested.

In the sixteenth and early part of the seventeenth century the Inns of Court appear to have arranged their Christmas festivities with a total disregard of expense. In 1535 a Mr. Francis Vivian, who was " Christmas Prince " of the Middle Temple, is said to have spent the equivalent of £2000 in this manner.[1] During the Twelve Days of Christmas he maintained all the state of an actual sovereign; dined daily in the hall under a " Cloth of Estate "; being saluted by his chaplains in church with three low bows; receiving petitions, which he handed to his Master of Requests; and finally conferring several mock knighthoods.

The following are the titles assumed by one who played Lord of Misrule before Queen Elizabeth in 1594: " The high and mighty Prince Henry, Prince of Purpoole, Archduke of Stapulia and Bernardin, Duke of High and Nether Holborn, Marquis of St. Giles and Tottenham, Count Palatine of Bloomsbury and Clerkenwell, Great Lord of the Cantons of Islington, Kentish Town, Paddington, and Knightsbridge, Knight of the Most Heroical Order of the Helmet, and Sovereign of the same."

The " merry disports " of the Elizabethan age were characterized by much splendour, boundless extravagance, a considerable amount of humour, and occasional cruelty. This is scarcely to be wondered at, in a time when cock fighting and bull baiting were quite usual pastimes, and bear baiting was deemed worthy of royal countenance and patronage. We have a detailed account of the daily feasting and merry-making by the

[1] This may seem incredible; but Hone tells us (*Year Book*, p. 1503) that in the ninth year of Charles I the four Inns of Court provided a Christmas masque which cost £2400.

members of the Inner Temple during the Twelve
Days of one Elizabethan Christmas. On St. Stephen's
Day, immediately before dinner, there was a pageant
in the Hall in which various great officers of state were
personated. These were attended by sixteen trumpeters
and four drums and fifes, with other subordinates.
When these great officers were seated at table, there
came in " The Master of the Game in green velvet,
and The Ranger of the Forest in green satin; each
bearing in his hand a green bow and divers arrows,
with each of them a hunting-horn about his neck, blowing together three blasts of venery ". These, having
marched thrice round the fire (which was evidently in
the middle of the hall), took their seats. Then came a
huntsman with a fox and a cat in a net, and with them
nine or ten couple of hounds; and forthwith the fox
and cat were worried to death by the hounds with
blowing of hunting-horns. After this " merry disport "
the company proceeded to dinner.

More respectable, probably less costly, and certainly
more conducive to honest mirth, was a pageant exhibited to the townsfolk of Norwich in 1640, by one John
Gladman, or, by another account, Hickman. Being
crowned as " King of Christmas ", he rode in state
through the city, dressed forth in silk and tinsel, preceded by twelve persons habited as the twelve months
of the year; and followed by " Lent, clothed in white
garments trimmed with herring skins, on a horse with
trappings of oyster shells, in token that sadness should
follow, and a holy time ". In this way they rode through
the streets, accompanied by many in grotesque dresses;
some in armour, carrying staves, and occasionally

engaging in mock combat; some as devils, chasing and frightening the children; and some in skin dresses, counterfeiting bears, wolves, lions, &c., and endeavouring to imitate their voices. This is the latest Christmas pageant of which we have any detailed account prior to the temporary ascendancy of Puritanism.

It is easy to understand that in an age when refinement was only to be found in a very limited section of the upper class, when the manners of the common people, however merry and picturesque, were on the whole extremely coarse, such organized revels would be apt to degenerate into rude practical joking and horseplay, and would generally tend to relax the bonds of social morality. It is not, therefore, wholly surprising to find a statute of the Scottish Parliament, passed in the year 1555, wherein " It is statute and ordained that in all times coming, na manner of person be chosen Robert Hude, nor Littlejohn, Abbot of Unreason, Queen's of May, or otherwise, nouther in burgh nor to landwart, in onie time to come ". Provosts, baillies, &c., electing such personages were to lose their municipal freedom for five years; electors not in burghs to be fined ten pounds and be imprisoned during the Queen's pleasure; " and the acceptor of sic-like office sall be banished foorth of the realm ".[1]

After the Restoration the Lord of Misrule seems to have had a temporary resuscitation at the Inns of Court; Evelyn tells of being " invited to the solemn foolery " at Lincoln's Inn on 1st January, 1662, and

---

[1] Sir Walter Scott narrates, in note H to *The Abbot*, that in 1561 the provost and two bailies of Edinburgh actually sentenced James Gillion, a cobbler, to be hanged for acting the part of Robin Hood in a pageant. John Knox, then in the height of his power, declined to interfere; and hanged thé poor man would have been but for a forcible rescue, under circumstances which amounted to a serious riot.

Pepys mentions the presence of the king there on the following day. But the revival seems only to have been transient.

Many defunct elements in the old-fashioned Christmas we may view with sentimental regret. Some we may hopefully endeavour to revive, as we have already welcomed back the Queen of the May. But we will shed no tear over the Lord of Misrule or Abbot of Unreason. Let him rest in peace:

> " If there were aught for us to wail
> 'T would be his resurrection ".

38. YULE-FIRTH: " UNTHRIFTY FOLK "

Before the Reformation there was in Scotland and the north of England a custom of great but uncertain antiquity called " Yule-firth ", i.e. " Christmas Truce ". Where this prevailed no criminal prosecution could be initiated in the week immediately preceding Christmas; and during the week next following all legal proceedings were temporarily suspended in honour of the feast.

Of the extent to which Yule-firth was observed we have no information; but something may be said in this connection of a strange custom at York, of which the earliest definite mention is found about the time of Henry VIII. On St. Thomas's Day the Sheriff made proclamation at the pillory that, during the Twelve Days of Christmas, all manner of thieves, gamblers, loose women, " and all other unthrifty folk be welcome to the town, whether they come late or early, in reverence of the High Feast of Yule "; on condition, however, that they kept the king's peace and submitted to certain police regulations. How long this custom survived is uncertain; but a writer in the middle of the eighteenth century refers to it as " not long discontinued ".

It would be pleasant if we could accept as historic the very beautiful symbolism which a lady has lately read into the strange custom. Adopting the Neo-Druidic idea that the parasitical mistletoe represents man in his dependence on God, she associates the York invitation to all and sundry with the ceremonial placing of mistletoe on the altar in the cathedral; and sees in it an object lesson that only when man lays himself on the altar as ready for sacrifice, can pardon, freedom, and true life be fully enjoyed. But it is more likely, we think, that the authorities at York were of opinion that by giving these " unthrifty folk " temporary security against arrest, they might the better be kept under observation, and their depredations guarded against. Municipal regulation of vice, however, always has tended and always will tend to deterioration of public morals; and we can very well believe that the York proclamation, like the unseemly pranks of the Lord of Misrule, did much to prepare the way towards the austerity of Puritan reaction.

39. CHRISTMAS GIFTS— SANTA CLAUS, ETC.

It seems only reasonable that the festival which commemorates the Supreme Gift of Divine Love should be a time for the interchange of gifts between kinsfolk and friends, as well as of bountiful alms to the poor.

The customs and traditions relating to Christmas gifts are many and various; some superstitious, some merely droll, and some instinct with poetic beauty. It may be as well to begin with those associated with St. Nicholas.

Nicholas lived about the beginning of the fourth century. He was Bishop of Myra, a coast town of Lycia, almost equidistant from the nearest points of Rhodes and Cyprus. Being rich, there was nothing he liked better than helping people who were in distress; and being modest there was nothing he hated so much as being thanked for it. So it happened again and again that a poor family who were in desperate need would find a gold piece or a well-filled purse that came from nobody knew where. At length the secret benefactor was discovered, and from that day to this, when people have received welcome gifts from unknown sources, St. Nicholas has had the credit of it.

Moreover, St. Nicholas was regarded as the special patron of boys; the boy-bishop was elected on his feast-day; and with good reason, if we may believe his legend. A wicked innkeeper had murdered two boys, and, being as greedy as he was cruel, had salted them down for pork. St. Nicholas, coming that way, inquired for the youngsters, and was told that they had gone out. He suggested that if such were the fact their mother was not aware of it, and promptly put the matter to the test. Being a saint, of course, he possessed the power of working miracles; so he made the sign of the cross over the pickle-tub, and out came the two boys, as lively as ever, and none the worse for their adventure. We may imagine the confusion of the naughty vintner; and may hope that he was converted by the miracle, and continued a good Catholic to the end of his days.

In Holland and Germany the benevolent saint is familiarly known as " Santa Claus ". He was introduced into England as the secret dispenser of Christmas gifts in the latter part of the eighteenth century. It is said that his familiar title was really imported from America, where it had already been naturalized by Dutch settlers. The suspending of a stocking as a receptacle for the expected gifts was accounted for by an absurd story that St. Nicholas, on one of his midnight expeditions, climbed on a roof, and dropped a purse down the chimney; which, instead of falling on the hearth, fell into a stocking that was hung up to dry!

In the Black Forest (in Germany) the annual visit of Santa Claus is preceded by that of Knecht Rupert, who goes round the village in a frightful disguise, visiting every house, and terrifying the naughty children by his preternatural acquaintance with their various misdemeanours. He generally concludes with an intimation that Santa Claus will be merciful this time, but if they do not grow better by next year the consequences may be unpleasant.

In Norway Santa Claus has so many presents to deliver that he needs the assistance of his servant Kris Kringle,[1] who conveys the delightful load over the roofs of the houses in a reindeer sleigh, which runs so lightly because it was built in Fairyland.

As St. Nicholas was the special patron of boys, St. Lucy was the special guardian of girls. Her feast day was on 13th December (the shortest day of the un-

---

[1] The name seems to be a corruption of *Christkindlein*, i.e. " Little Christ-child ".

reformed calendar), on which day torch-light processions were held, schools were illuminated, and it was
usual to shoot and fish by torchlight. St. Lucy was a
Sicilian maiden, martyred about the year 304. Her
legend is that a rejected suitor denounced her to the
authorities as a Christian, whereupon she was tortured,
had her eyes put out, and was put to death. Later and
absurd stories arose from the custom of painting her
as carrying her eyes in a dish!

In Switzerland Father Christmas, with jovial red
face and white beard, and clad in a long furred robe,
marches round the village with his wife Lucy. She
wears a round cap over her long plaits of hair, a smart
laced bodice, and a silk apron. She distributes gifts to
the girls, while her husband looks after the boys.

In Sweden St. Lucy was personated by the prettiest
girl in the house, dressed in white with a red sash;
having on her head a wire crown covered with bilberry
twigs, in which were fixed nine candles. She went
through the house at the first cock-crowing, and
wakened all the sleepers, offering to each a cup of
coffee or sweet drink. When all were dressed, breakfast was taken in a room brilliantly lighted.

In the Boehmer-wald St. Lucy is a bogie, who
appears in the form of a nanny-goat with horns; gives
fruit to good children, and threatens to rip up the
naughty ones. In Russia the gifts are credited to the
Babuska, i.e. the Grandmother; an old woman who,
when the wise men from the East inquired the way,
wilfully misdirected them. According to another version, each of them in succession urged her to go with
him to visit the new-born King, but she would not

Christmas Gifts

go until she had finished her spinning. When, at
length, her task was done, she would have followed
them, but could not, for the snow had covered their
tracks. By yet another account, when the holy family
were going down into Egypt, she refused them hospitality. Whatever her fault was, she repented of her
unkindness; and ever since has been trying to make
amends by going round the world on Christmas Eve
distributing gifts to all good children.

In Germany in the sixteenth century Christmas
gifts for children were tied up in bundles, which contained " something pleasant, something useful, and
something pertaining to discipline ": for example, cake,
sugar-plums, money, a garment, a book, pen, or paper,
and always a twig, suggestive of the rod. They were
supposed to be brought by " der Haus-Christ ". In
modern Germany the old tradition of *das Christ-kind*
is often sadly perverted; He is actually personated, in
a fashion wholly unlike the Child of Bethlehem; something between the Divine Infant and an angel, but more
like a good fairy than either. He is often a tall child,
probably a girl, with long fair hair, and dressed in white.
In Alsace it is usually a girl, with a crown of gilt paper
and lighted candles, having in one hand a silver bell,
and in the other a basket of sweets. She is attended by
Hans Trapp, in a bear-skin, with a long beard and a
rod. He threatens the naughty children, who are saved
by the intercession of *das Christ-kind*. Sometimes the
attendant is *der Schimmel-reiter*, who on entering jumps
over a chair, and dances with one of the girls. Meanwhile *das Christ-kind* makes the children recite a hymn
or some verses of Scripture; if they do it well *Christ-*

kind rewards them with gingerbread; if badly he beats them with a bag filled with ashes. Then he and *Schimmel-reiter* dance and pass on.

In France and Germany the usual receptacle for Christmas gifts is a wooden shoe. If in the shoe a small faggot should be found, the recipient would understand that Santa Claus's verdict was " Not deserving ". But he would probably find some mitigation in the shape of a concealed packet of bon-bons.

In Sweden, as also in Pomerania and some other parts of Germany, a small and valuable Christmas gift, such as a jewel or a ring, is made up into a large bundle, the " Yule-Klapp ", which takes both time and labour to unpack. Stories are told, moreover, of ladies receiving a huge bundle from which, when opened, the donor himself emerged, like Cleopatra from the carpet—probably well assured beforehand that he would not be rejected.

In many parts of France " Noël ", the festival of good news, is personified, and the gifts are brought by Father Christmas himself. In other parts, especially in Brittany, they are directly ascribed to " Le Bon Jésus ", the Good Jesus, as in like manner in Germany the giver is *das Christ-kind*, the Christ-Child. And surely this is better than the fictitious Babuska, and Kris Kringle, and Knecht Rupert, and Santa Claus: better, because truer; for is not the Holy Child the real giver of whatever is given in honour of His blessed Nativity? Children are naturally imaginative, and apt to fear whatever is not understood. So it has happened that parents have kept up the old fables until the children, though eagerly expecting the presents that were to be brought by the mysterious nocturnal visitant, were afraid to sleep through dread of something ghostly. There was but one way to banish that fear; namely, to annihilate the little romance, and convince them that Santa Claus was really one whom they knew quite well by the name of " Mother ".

40. THE CHRISTMAS SHEAF

In Norway, Sweden, Denmark, and Hungary there is a regular custom of setting a small sheaf of corn on a pole in the gable of the house or barn; and he would be thought a very curmudgeon who would refuse the birds their Christmas feast. The boys in Denmark say " It is for Santa Claus's white horse "; and this is suggestive of what probably originated the custom. There can be little doubt that it is a pre-Christian survival, and that the sheaf was at first intended for Odin's horse Sleipnor.

But in the northern countries generally there is a prevailing notion that the lower animals ought to have a share in the Christmas bounty. St. Francis wished the oxen and asses to have extra hay and corn at Christmas, " for reverence of the Son of God, whom on such a night the blessed Virgin Mary did lay down in the stall between the ox and the ass ". He thought that " All Creation " should rejoice at Christmas, and the dumb creatures had no other means of doing so. Accordingly in Silesia wheat is given to the beasts on Christmas Eve " to make them thrive ". It was said that " If wheat be kept in one's pocket during Christmas service, and then given to the fowls, they will

grow fat and lay many eggs ". This seems to belong
to the large class of magical superstitions, according to
which a blessing or a curse is conveyed by means of
enchanted food or drink. In Norway there is usually
a great brewing beforehand of Yule ale, of which a
good portion is given to the cattle. This seems quite in
the spirit of Francis. Even more so is a custom which
is not yet quite extinct in the west of England. On
Christmas Day a double ration of provender is given
to horses and other cattle " for luck "; and it is said
that if this were neglected misfortune would certainly
follow. Akin to this is a custom in some parts of Italy
and Spain of scattering grain on Christmas Eve as a
feast for the birds.

41. THE CHRISTMAS TREE

Nothing in connection with Christmas gifts is more
popular than the Christmas tree, with which, however, it is by no means certain that they were at first
related. Its origin is very obscure, " lost in the mazes
of antiquity ". Some folk-lorists think it had to do
with the worship or invocation of the " spirit of vegetation ", and relate it to other ceremonial trees, such
as the May Pole, or the St. John's tree of the Erzgebirge, around which the people danced at the summer
solstice. Some associate it with a story of St. Boniface
(otherwise Winfrid of Crediton, an English missionary
in Germany in the eighth century), who is said to have
cut down on a Christmas Eve a sacred oak, beneath
which human sacrifices had been offered: as it fell
a young fir tree seemed to appear miraculously beyond

it; and this, unstained with blood, the saint proposed as a sign or emblem of the new faith. Others connect the Christmas tree with an old legend about a marvellous transformation of nature at the birth of our Lord, when the rivers flowed with wine, and the trees blossomed in the midst of ice and snow.

With this legend may be associated a custom in Austria, Carinthia, and Tyrol; where boughs of cherry, pear, or hawthorn are gathered early in December, and put in water or wet sand indoors, that they may blossom at Christmas. Akin to this may be what we read of in London in the fifteenth century, when holm, holly, ivy, and bay were made into a standard tree on Cornhill. Half a century later " a tree of gold " appeared in a Christmas pageant presented before King Henry VIII. Although there is neither record nor probable tradition as to the origin of the Christmas tree, there is a pretty German folk-tale on the subject that is worth the telling. On a stormy Christmas Eve a forester and his household had made fast the door, and gathered around a cheerful fire. By and by knocking was heard outside, and the housefather, opening the door, saw a little child, cold, hungry, and all but exhausted. He was kindly welcomed, warmed and fed, and little Hans insisted on giving up his bed to the stranger. In the morning the family were aroused by the singing of a choir of angels; and, looking at their unbidden guest, they saw him transfigured, for He was none other than the Christ-Child. He broke off a branch from a fir tree, and set it in the earth. " See," (said He) " I have gladly received your gifts, and this is My gift to you. Henceforward this tree shall always bear its fruit at Christmas, and you shall always have abundance." There can be no need to elaborate the meaning of this story if we remember Who it was that said, " Inasmuch as ye have done it to one of the least of these, ye did it unto Me ".

The Christmas tree, as we know it, is first met with in Germany about the time of Luther. Popular tradition, which though not corroborated by evidence is not therefore necessarily incredible, ascribes its introduction to the Great Reformer himself; but the earliest definite mention of it as an established custom is in an anonymous MS. dated 1605. It does not seem to have been generally common till far into the eighteenth century: it was sooner popular in Protestant than in Roman Catholic communities; and until quite lately it scarcely existed in some rural parts of Bavaria. Originally a purely domestic institution, it gradually found its way first into Protestant and then into Catholic churches; and at Munich it has even invaded the cemetery, where on Christmas Eve the graves are decked with holly and mistletoe, and sometimes a little Christmas tree with its gleaming lights.

Leisurely as was the progress of this pleasant custom, by the middle of last century the Christmas tree had become almost universal throughout Germany. It was set up in almost every house, rich and poor, even where there were only elderly people. From thence it spread throughout the greater part of Christendom. It is said to have been adopted in Finland about 1800, and was known in Denmark and Norway in 1830. The very first Christmas tree in England is said to have been set up at Penshanger in 1829, by a German lady,

Princess Lieven. This was altogether an exotic, and the tree was only naturalized in England after it had been set up at Windsor Castle by Prince Albert in 1841. In the same year it is said to have been introduced into Paris; and fifty years later, between 30,000 and 35,000 trees were sold in that city in one season. It seems doubtful if it was common in Bohemia or in Sweden much before 1860: previously, in the last-named country, it was customary to set up a bare pole outside the house, not very unlike the Asherah forbidden in the law of Moses. Since then the Christmas tree has found a welcome in Holland, Switzerland, Italy, Spain, Austria, Russia, and America; largely through German influence, direct or indirect.

It is not difficult to conceive that the Christmas tree may have been originally an embodiment of the Spirit of Vegetation, and may have been Christianized by association with the beautiful old legend of the Tree of Life. When Adam was dying, says the story, he sent Seth to the garden of Eden to beg for the Oil of Mercy. This he could not obtain; but the guardian cherub gave him instead a sprig, or a seed, from the Tree of Life, which he was commanded to plant upon his father's grave. He did so; and therefrom grew a tree which in after ages afforded the wonder-working rod of Moses. Later it was cut down and cast away; but just because it had been thus rejected, it was taken up and fashioned into the very cross on which our Lord was crucified, and so became the Tree of Life indeed.

That the Christmas tree was adorned with lights in, or soon after, Luther's time is certain; how soon it became the vehicle of gifts is more doubtful. To this day in Germany gifts of a utilitarian character are never hung on the tree, but placed on a table beside it. In Denmark, where the tree has become as popular as in Germany, there is a pleasant custom that on returning from church on Christmas Eve the whole family, including servants and visitors, join hands and march round the tree singing carols. The favourite carol on this occasion is the old macaronic " A Child is born in Bethlehem ".

In some parts of Germany the tree is made to typify the Stem of Jesse—the human genealogy of our Lord. Adam and Eve stand at the foot; the serpent is twined round the stem; but at the top is a light, brighter than all the rest—the Light of the World, the Seed of the woman who should bruise the Serpent's head.

In recent years an interesting development of the old custom has appeared in America. In several cities a municipal Christmas tree has been set up in some open square or other public place, where it affords a gratuitous entertainment for the poor.

Another modern American adaptation makes the tree a central feature in a distinctly religious service. The church is darkened, except for the dim light of two candles on opposite sides. The psalm " Out of the depths " (130th) is sung; and then various Messianic prophecies are recited, each by a separate voice. At each recitation a taper is lighted on the tree, till the whole is illuminated. Then the Gospel narrative is recited in like manner, each section being followed by a hymn or carol, treated as a solo, trio, or quartet:

the service ends with a hymn sung by the entire con-
gregation, and the recital of the words of our Lord,
" I am the Light of the World, &c.". This Tree-
Lighting service is said to have been introduced by a
minister who had seen something of a similar character
in Spain. It seems very like a festal inversion of the
" Tenebræ ", sung in Roman Catholic churches in the
Holy Week.

Like many other foreign importations, the Christmas tree has often been sadly bungled by English
commercialism, and so completely robbed of its beautiful significance. The tree of bazaars and fancy fairs,
with its load of toys to be *sold* off, or allotted to *purchasers*
of numbered tickets, is about as unlike the real thing as
it well could be. The very essence of the symbolism
is that the glittering fruit is a gift, not a purchase;
and—which is not less important—that it rises over
the crib wherein lay the Babe of Bethlehem. For the
Christmas tree is the Tree of Life. Let it arise in its
evergreen verdure, bright with tapers, and bending
down with treasures to be—not sold—but given as freely
as the grace of God. Let the Christmas angel appear
at the summit, and at its foot the Manger, out of which
grows the unfading Tree. And so let the children learn
from this beautiful object lesson, that all things bright
and sweet and precious are the Gifts of the Holy Child
Jesus.

42. THE CHRISTMAS SHIP

Closely allied to the Christmas tree is another old
German custom, scarcely yet naturalized among us:
the *Christmas Ship*. Of its origin we have no account—

neither record nor tradition. In Greece, in heathen times, a ship was carried in procession in honour of the wine-god Dionysus; and still at Athens the waits carry about models of warships at the New Year, it is said in honour of St. Basil, whose feast is kept on 1st January, and who is said to have set out on a voyage on that day. But it is hard to say what Greek influence could have operated in Germany in the early Middle Ages. The association of a ship with Christmas, as the bearer of precious things from afar, is indicated in the old doggerel " I saw three ships come sailing by on Christmas day in the morning ". This seems to have some genealogical relation to a sixteenth-century carol of which a fragment runs:

> " There came a ship far sailing then,
>   St. Michael was the steersman,
>   St. John sat in the horn;
>   Our Lord harped, our Lady sang,
>   And all the bells of heaven rang
>   On Christmas in the morn."

But these are faint and broken echoes of a noble original—that sweet carol which we owe to the great mediæval mystic John Tauler of Strasburg (died, 1361), and of which the Christmas ship, laden with toys, is a visible embodiment:

> " There comes a galley sailing,
>   With amplest cargo stored;
>   It bears God's Son most loving,
>   The Lord's Eternal Word.
>
> " That galley, calmly floating,
>   Bears freight of priceless cost;

Love is the sail that wafts it;
　Its mast, the Holy Ghost.

·" The earth now holds the anchor;
　The ship to land hath won;
God's Word our flesh hath taken,
　To mankind comes the Son.

" In Bethlehem an Infant,
　Born in a manger-stall,
He gives Himself to save us;
　Then praise Him, one and all.

" And whoso seeks that Infant
　With loving clasp to hold,
Must first with Him bear anguish
　And sorrows manifold;

" And then, with Jesus dying,
　Again with Jesus rise,
An heir of life eternal,
　Where Jesus gives the prize."

43. CHRISTMAS BOXES

In taking leave of Christmas gifts, we naturally
think of the gifts to children at the Roman *Sigillaria*,
and of the *Strenæ* offered to the Emperor, or exchanged
between private citizens on the Kalends of January.
" Men gave sweet things, that the year might be full
of sweetness; lamps, that it might be full of light;
coin, that wealth might flow in amain ": evidently a
sort of sympathetic magic to ensure a lucky New Year.
It is easy to see how a New Year's custom might be
transferred to Christmas; but not so easy to under-

stand why the seasonable gift should be expected on the day following the feast, or why that day should be called Boxing Day. Indeed there is no man living who certainly *knows*, though many have *guessed*, the origin and primary meaning of " Boxing Day " and " Christmas Box ".

Most folk-lorists associate the words with the earthen savings-box which had to be broken to release its hoard. It is well known that servants and apprentices, especially London apprentices, used such boxes to collect those Christmas gifts which they deemed their legitimate perquisites. Naturally the box would be broken only when fully charged, i.e. when Christmas Day was past. An essayist, writing in 1621, says of a covetous man " as an apprentice's box of earth, apt he is to take all, but to restore none till he be broken ". Another, under date 1642, makes the same comparison, phrasing it thus: " like the Christmas earthen boxes of apprentices ". Wither alludes to the earthen box in that merry song of his which has furnished so many seasonable proverbs; but he seems rather to be thinking of savings accumulated in the past, and now made available to *prepare* for the feast:

> " Our kitchen-boy has broke his box;
> And to the dealing of the ox
> Our honest neighbours come by flocks,
> Because they will be merry."

A hundred years later Henry Carey introduced the same idea in his delightfully humorous ballad of " Sally in our Alley ". He makes his London 'prentice say:

" Oh, Christmas time is drawing near,
    And then I shall have money;
I 'll save it up, and, box and all,
    I 'll give it to my honey."

The earthen box for savings is still to be found in Holland, where it is commonly made in the shape of a pig, and is called " The Feast Pig ". To break it unseasonably is unlucky; almost a crime according to the ethics of the nursery.

Another explanation of the familiar phrase makes it refer to the church alms-box, the contents of which were not dispensed until the day after Christmas, which was therefore called Boxing Day.

Others say that the words have nothing to do with a box of any kind; that they came hither with the Crusaders, and are nothing else but the Arabic *Backsheesh*, i.e. a gratuity. There is not much of history to support this view of the matter; but one might almost be tempted to adopt it in view of the fact that of old—and indeed not so very long since—every person who had or was supposed to have rendered any service to another during the year looked for backsheesh at Christmas, indeed regarded it as a right. Husk says: " Every householder was duly waited upon by the postman, the lamplighter, the waits, the turncock, the parish beadle, the dustman, the parish watchman, and others ". In London the parish beadles, who usually exercised the function of town criers, were accustomed about Christmas time to distribute a list of the parish officers for the year, and other information, with an appeal to public generosity in doggerel rhyme more or less seasonable. Specimens of such " bellman's verses " are known of date 1735; and one firm, Reynells of Piccadilly, afterwards of Little Pultney Street, continued to produce them for at least 130 years. Husk tells us that " a heavy blow and great discouragement to the custom of Christmas boxing among tradesmen has been given by the growing practice of keeping the shops closed on Boxing Day". No one, unless it were Mr. Scrooge before his conversion, would grudge a Christmas box to the postman, the lamplighter, or the dustman; but it is a different matter when servants claim backsheesh from tradesmen who supply their masters, or clerks and managers of retail traders expect presents from the wholesale dealers.

Be that as it may, the best kind of Christmas box, that which is most in accord with the genius of the season, is one recommended as long ago as the days of Nehemiah: " Go your way, eat of the fat and drink of the sweet, and send portions to those for whom nothing is provided ".

Before finally dismissing the topic of Christmas gifts, it may be well to mention the publication of seasonable gift-books, which for a century and a half have been growing, year by year, more and more luxurious. They were originally designed for children and were of a very simple character. The earliest examples known are those issued by John Newbury, the famous bookseller of St. Paul's Churchyard, in 1765; one of which is *The History of Goody Two-shoes*, ascribed, on what seems to be satisfactory evidence, to Oliver Goldsmith.

THE FIRST CHRISTMAS CARD (1846)

From a facsimile of the original design made by J. C. Horsley, R.A., for Sir Henry Cole.

44. CHRISTMAS CARDS, ETC.

It might seem like an oversight if nothing were said of the pretty social custom of Christmas cards, albeit they are of quite modern origin. There must be many aged persons who can remember their first appearance; and some, perhaps, have preserved specimens of the earliest issues. There is some uncertainty as to the date when the *first* Christmas card was actually sent. Some ascribe the invention to Mr. W. C. T. Dobson, R.A., who, it is said, in December, 1844, sent to a friend a sketch symbolizing the spirit of Christmas, and in the following year designed another card, of which he sent lithographed copies to numerous friends and acquaintances. Others say that the initiative belongs to Mr. J. C. Horsley, who in 1846 dispatched a card which is described as "an elaborate affair, showing two allegorical designs of clothing the naked and feeding the hungry, together with a family group of three generations, quaffing wine". It was some time before the cards were put on the market. Unless our memory is much at fault, they were first sold about 1858 or 1859, and were not common till 1862. The earlier types were very simple: a cock-robin, or a sprig of holly or mistletoe, with a conventional greeting. Year by year they grew more and more artistic, until about 1883 or 1884 they reached their acme of pictorial beauty and seasonable fitness. Nothing since has ever surpassed a triptych in the style of early Florentine art, which was published about that time. In the centre was the Holy Family, with patriarchs and prophets behind, the shepherds and mage-kings adoring in front, singing angels overhead, and in the wings the apostles and other saints, typical of the Holy Catholic Church in all the ages. Since then there has been artistic decline, art becoming more and more subservient to the demands of trade and the perpetual craving for novelty. The individual greeting-cards have tended in the same direction. Year by year the colour-printers give us cards which from a merely decorative point of view are as beautiful as ever, but except for the lettering most of them would be just as well suited to May Day or Michaelmas.

Space must be found for mention of an obsolete custom which arose in schools early in the eighteenth century. This was the production of " Christmas Pieces "—specimens of handwriting laboriously produced under the superintendence of the writing-master, to show what progress had been made by the pupil in the last twelve months. Husk had a collection of these " Pieces ", forming an almost unbroken series from 1720 to 1840. They were on large sheets of superior writing-paper, with engraved borders, a blank being left in the middle for the specimen penmanship. Husk says that the early engravings were often of considerable merit, but they became by degrees poorer and poorer. They were supposed to represent some important event of the year, as a battle, a coronation, an earthquake, &c., or scenes illustrating rural sports, military exercises, Bartholomew Fair, and the like. Scripture subjects were sometimes adopted, but rarely at first. About 1805 colour was introduced, and about 1820 it became general; Scripture subjects, too, supplanted other designs. From this time the engraving deteriorated: respectable copper-plate gave place to mere outlines as a guide to the colourist, and these to common woodcuts, and finally to ornate " Flourishes " from the pen of the writing-master. But long before they ceased to be sold, the use of these " Christmas Pieces " was discontinued in all schools of the better class. The custom was dying out in the boyhood of the present writer, who still remembers that its unpleasant associations made the near prospect of the holidays more delightful.

FAMILY REUNIONS—THE CHILDREN'S DAY

Many of our social and domestic customs are a natural recognition of the *new order* which the Babe of Bethlehem introduced into the world. There can surely be nothing worthy the name of a Christian celebration of the feast if it be not associated with the clearing off of old scores, the payment—as far as possible—of our just debts, the forgiving of debtors who through honest poverty are unable to pay, and the laying aside of old grudges and quarrels. Yet it is to be feared that some of us have not quite outgrown the need of that lesson which Dickens taught in the immortal *Christmas Carol* of 1843.

Then our *family reunions* tell very eloquently of the revelation of human brotherhood by Him who " showed us the Father ", and contracted a fraternal relationship with the whole human race.

And we feel, too, that Christmas is peculiarly the

Children's Day. One of our most genial humorists has touched a true chord when, personifying the day as usual, he says:

" Christmas comes, he comes, he comes,
    Ushered in with a rain of plums;
    Hollies in the windows greet him,
    Schools come driving post to meet him,
    Gifts precede him, bells proclaim him,
    Every voice delights to name him.

" Curtains, those snug room-enfolders
    Hang upon his million shoulders;
    And he has a million eyes
    Of fire, and eats a million pies,
    And is very merry and wise—
    Very wise and very merry,
    And loves a kiss beneath the berry.

" And he would have us, one and all,
    Awake at his benignant call,
    And all be wise, and all lay down
    Strife, and jealousy, and frown,
    And, like the sons of one great mother,
    Share and be blest with one another."

In Norway there is a pleasant way of impressing on the children that it is their own day, the birthday of their own Divine Brother, by a custom which is evidently a Christianized survival of one that has been already mentioned in connection with Christmas ghosts. The ghosts in Norwegian farm-houses have long been laid, but still the children do not go to bed on Christmas Eve. After supper, straw is laid down in the house-place, and there the children sleep that night.[1] They

---

[1] A good deal of superstition is, or was, connected with this " Yule Straw ". It was put in the nesting-places of fowls to protect them from witches; or given to cattle, before driving them to summer pasture, as a charm against sickness or accident.

are thus reminded of the tender sympathy of
Father with the little children, even with the lo
the poor. It is well for us to think of this; of t
Child, not merely as lying in the manger, or ͨᵃʳʳⁱᵉᵈ
into Egypt to escape from the cruelty of Herod, but as
playing with the boys in the street of Nazareth, or
among the chips and shavings in the carpenter's shop.
It is well to sing, once a year,

> " Backward, turn backward, O years in your flight;
> Make me a child again, just for to-night."

46. MISCELLANEOUS CHRISTMAS SUPERSTITIONS, ETC.

Before passing on to the traditions and customs of
the twelve days following Christmas, it will be convenient to bring together a number of superstitions
that cannot easily be classified.

One of them is the widespread belief that as midnight ushers in the Holy Birth-tide the cattle fall on
their knees in honour of Him who lay in the manger.
It is said that the Christianized Indians in America
believe that at the same time the deer kneel in worship
of the Great Spirit. And it is an undeniable fact that
cattle often have been seen on their knees on Christmas
Eve. In Somerset this was referred to *Old* Christmas
Eve (5–6th January), when " the Master Ox lowed
softly three times, and then kneeled towards the
manger ". It seems a pity to spoil a poetic legend with
a prosaic comment; but the simple truth is that *all*
ruminant animals, oxen, sheep, deer, camels, and the
rest, when arising from a recumbent posture, almost

always get first on their knees—or in other words " get up hind legs first ".

Somewhat akin to the belief in the kneeling oxen is a tradition, current in the Greek Orthodox Church, that on Christmas Eve all trees and plants, especially those on the banks of the Jordan, bow in reverence to the Saviour. A man rode into Lydda shortly before midnight on Christmas Eve, and tethered his ass to a prostrate palm tree, which he supposed had been blown down by the wind. In the morning the tree stood erect, and the poor ass was effectually hanged— a plain proof that the Greek Calendar was right, and the Reformed Calendar of the West entirely wrong.

A less pleasing superstition once prevailed in some parts of England, France, and Germany. It was believed that on this one night of all the year oxen were able to speak. Many tales were said to have been overheard when the oxen were talking, but " the listeners never heard any good of themselves ". The bovine utterances usually had something to do with sudden death.

In Scotland, before the Reformation, it was customary to visit the byre and stable on Christmas Eve, and there say an *Ave Maria* and a *Paternoster* to safeguard the cattle and horses from the evil eye. There was also a pretty fancy that bees might be heard singing in the hive on Christmas Eve.

Another old superstition was related to the *gambling* which too frequently mingled with the Christmas sport. Kirchmeyer, describing the customs of his day in the Roman Catholic parts of Germany, tells us that at the midnight and early morning masses the people's offerings were severally laid on the altar, and some

" The money still do watch
That first to altar comes, which then they privily do snatch;
The priest, lest other should it have, takes oft the same away,
Whereby they think throughout the year to have good luck in
    play ".

Other superstitions have to do with divination. Great importance used to attach to the day of the week on which Christmas fell. From this was prognosticated the prevalent weather, and the fruitfulness or unfruitfulness of the ensuing season, the fortunes of those born on that day, the recovery or death of those who on that day fell sick, &c. An elaborate rhyming guide on the subject is contained in one of the Harleian MSS. in the British Museum,[1] from which the appropriate stanza is often quoted as a curiosity in the Christmas papers.

Another form of divination was distinctly funny. A girl *knocked loudly at the sty door* on Christmas Eve; if a great hog first grunted in reply, her predestined husband would be an old man; if it were a little pig, that gave promise of a young one.

A characteristic Yorkshire superstition about *First Footings* is probably not yet quite extinct. It relates to the person who first enters the house on Christmas Morning. A woman or a girl is thought to bring ill fortune; a man or boy usually brings good luck, but he must always bring something into the house, if it be only a sprig of holly, before anything is taken out. It is also held that a dark-haired lad ensures better luck

[1] Harl. MS. 2252.

than one who is fair. This may be a trace of race-antagonism, inherited from a time when the dark-haired Briton was a more welcome guest than the fair-haired Saxon. This explanation is favoured by another superstition, that *a flat-footed person* brings ill luck: and it is said that, on an average, Welshmen are higher in the instep than Englishmen.

In Scotland nothing was to be taken out of the house on Christmas Day, unless as a present. Some-what akin to this was the belief that the luckiest person in the house during the next year would be he or she who first opened the door " to let Christmas in ". The proper way to do it is to open the door wide, and say, " Welcome, Father Christmas ".

The chirping of a *cricket* at Christmas was widely believed to portend good luck; but to bring into the house anything made of *leather* was very unlucky.

The Glastonbury Legend is well known. The story is that Joseph of Arimathea and his comrades, fatigued with their journey, sat down to rest on Weary-all Hill, where Joseph set his staff in the ground. It took root, and became a hawthorn tree; which always " blossomed at Christmas, mindful of its Lord ", until it was cut down by a Puritan in the days of Queen Elizabeth. Several trees, grown from the haws of the sacred thorn, still flourish in the neighbourhood, and have the like virtue; only they bloom at Twelfth-tide, which proves that the Reformed Calendar is not yet accepted in Wonderland. The local form of the legend is that the trees, being already in bud, unfold their blooms at midnight on the 5–6th January, but after a short time close them again. Within living memory many persons made a nocturnal pilgrimage to one or other of these holy trees, in hope to see the miracle. The simple fact is that about Glastonbury, as elsewhere, there is a number of pink hawthorns the original stock of which was imported from the East, and which usually bloom in the winter.

A Yorkshire saying, probably not so much a super-stition as a kindly jest, is that " In as many houses as you eat a mince pie in the twelve days of Christmas, so many happy months you will have in the year ". One thing is certain, the more of the true Christmas spirit we cultivate the more happiness we shall enjoy all the year round.

There is an Irish superstition that the gates of Paradise are always open at midnight on Christmas Eve; so that anyone dying at that moment enters at once, without going to Purgatory. Grim stories are told of persons who were obviously dying, and were kindly helped out of this world just at the critical moment.

In some places there was a notion that it was un-lucky to be born on Christmas Eve; there was danger that the unfortunate wight would become a werewolf! As a counterpart to this we may mention a Scottish belief that " those born on Christmas Eve or Good Friday have the power of seeing spirits, and even of commanding them ".

Another quaint belief, in some mining districts, was that on Christmas Eve High Mass was sung by invisible choristers in the mine which contains the richest lode of ore, and which was preternaturally lighted up for the occasion. A strange survival of heathenism long persisted in some parts of Bohemia, and perhaps is not yet quite extinct. A portion of the Christmas fare is thrown into the wells, as an offering to the springs—or more probably to the Guardian Spirit of the springs—as a safeguard against drought.

The last superstition we need mention here is that of the *Christmas Angel*. It used to be believed that every Christmas Eve a number of angels were sent from heaven, commissioned each to awaken an infant from its first sleep and carry it to Paradise, there to sing a carol in honour of the Christ-Child.

Christianity having had its cradle in the northern hemisphere, it was inevitable that Christmas should gather around it the associations and customs of a winter festival. The more distinctly religious observances were easily transported to a southern latitude; but in the case of many social and festive traditions this was impossible. Nevertheless, Christmas is as merry under the Southern Cross as under Charles's Wain, but it is there essentially a summer holiday, associated with flowers and picnics. A couple of snatches of Antipodean verse may illustrate this aspect of the festive season. A poet of English birth, but Australian domicile, writes thus of Christmas Eve:

" Where the Fern-king holds his revels in his hidden courts
    of green,
  And the wire-grass weaves a curtain to enshrine the mystic
    scene;
  There I lingered in the gloaming of a sunny Christmas-tide;

There I lingered 'midst the shadows while the daylight waned
 and died:
There I mused, and dreamed, and pondered of the happy
 days of yore,
Ere my errant feet had wandered to this strange Australian
 shore."

His meditations are interrupted by a band of children singing a carol, which runs thus:

" Morning Star o'er Bethlehem shining,
 Guide us to His lowly bed;
Evening lights at day's declining
 Soft reveal His weary head;
Flowers that bloom 'mid thorn and briar
 Shadow forth His footsteps fair;
Birds' sweet song in tuneful choir
 Sing His love and guardian care."

47. YULE-TIDE IN THULE

Before treating of the subsidiary festivals which go to complete the Christmas cycle, it seems convenient to say something of the customs that prevailed a century ago in the northern islands, where Scottish Puritanism was strangely blended with survivals of Scandinavian heathenism. This topic is somewhat elaborately treated in *The Home of a Naturalist*, by B. Edmundson and J. M. E. Saxby; from which the following account is condensed.

The Yule-tide observances of Shetland seem to have had but little relation to the Nativity; being largely a survival from the old Norse festival of the returning sun. The few who observed Christmas as a Christian anniversary did so according to the Reformed Calendar;

but the popular Yule was 25th December, old style, equivalent to 5th January, new style.

The Yule feast needed serious preparation. Seven days earlier was " Tul-ya's E'en ", when the " Trows " or " Grey Folk " were thought to leave their underground abodes. These were elves or gnomes, resembling if not identical with the Trolls of Norse mythology, sportively malignant, and certain to do mischief at Yule-tide unless due precautions were taken by " saining " the house and its occupants. Two straws were placed across at the stile or other entrance to the stackyard; a hair was plucked from the tail of every cow and beast of burden, and these, plaited together, were placed over the door of the byre; and a blazing peat was carried through the barn and other outhouses. That night, called " Helya's Night ", after supper, the grandmother or oldest woman in the house would spread her hands over the bed of each child, reciting an incantation to this effect:

> " Mary, Mother, hold thy hand
>   Ever above our sleeping band:
>   Hold the lass and hold the wife,
>   Hold the bairn all its life;
>   Mary, Mother, hold thy hand
>   Round the infants in our land."

During this ceremony the grandsire should rake the burning peats on the hearth, reciting another charm, which is now unfortunately forgotten.

" Thamas-mass ", five days before Yule, was deemed peculiarly holy. No work and no amusement was allowed after sunset; if this rule were broken, ill luck would surely follow. The Sunday before Yule was " Byana's Sunday ". Half a cow's head was boiled and eaten for supper; the skull was cleaned, and, a candle being stuck in the eye-socket, it was put aside for later use.

On Yule Eve a round oat-cake was baked for each child, larger or smaller according to age. These cakes had a hole in the middle, and were pinched into points around the edges; probably a reminiscence of the " Sun Wheel ". After this everyone made a complete ablution, from head to foot, three live coals being dropped into the water as a charm against the Trows. A clean, and if possible, a new garment was put on in which to sleep; but before sleeping the house was made tidy, all soiled water thrown away, all unseemly things put out of sight, all locks opened, an iron or steel blade—much feared by the Trows—was laid on the table, and a lamp left burning all night.

Before daylight the gudeman lit the before-provided candle, and carried it around as he fed the beasts, giving them better food than usual. Breakfast was eaten by candlelight, as many candles as possible being provided. The meal was as sumptuous as means would permit, and concluded—at least in the better-class houses—with a draught of " Whipcol ". This consisted of the yolks of a dozen eggs, beaten up with a pound of sugar, half a pint of rum, and a quart of cream. There was a jest that it was the tipple of the gods and heroes at their Yule-feast in Walhalla.

The short daylight was spent by the men and boys in a game of football, Yule being the opening day of the season for that favourite sport. No work of any kind must be done, " Else muckle dule will be thy share, this year and mair ". Dinner was eaten at sun-set, as ponderously substantial as the breakfast, with as many dainties of all kinds as could be procured. The evening was devoted to dancing; but it was necessary first to " sain " the children against the malice of the Trows. There was a gruesome story of two bairns whom their mother left in bed, forgetting to say the charm when she went to dance in a neighbour's barn. Remembering her omission, she turned back to repair it, but the children had vanished, and the next day were found dead in a snowdrift. The Trows were fond of dancing, and would, if possible, intrude into the company of mortals during the Yule-tide festivities; but they always vanished if pious words were spoken. It was, however, dangerous to talk lightly of them.

From Yule to New Year's Day, O.S., no work must be done, else ill luck will follow through the year. Football by day and dancing in the evening furnished the principal occupations. But on " New'r'day " work of every kind must begin, if only for a few minutes; " everything pertaining to thrift was got under way to begin the year well ". Work and play went hand in hand till the O.S. Twelfth Day (17th January, N.S.), when there were social merry makings on an enlarged scale. At the close of the day all doors were opened, a great pretence was made of driving out invisible intruders, passages from the Bible were read or recited, and iron was ostentatiously displayed " to drive the Trows away ". And when the next day dawned, the Trows had vanished and " The Yules " were ended.

48. SUBSIDIARY FESTIVALS

We now come to deal with the subordinate festivals of the Christmas cycle, each of which has its own special folk-lore. It was thought that as the season of Advent, leading up to Christmas, represents the coming of God to men, the twelve days following Christmas, and culminating in Epiphany, represented the coming of man to God. In England, during the Saxon monarchy, it was ordained by law that these twelve days should be kept holy; an ordinance which, like almost every other good thing of that age, was popularly ascribed to Alfred the Great.[1]

Boxing Day has been already referred to in connection with Christmas boxes; but from the latter part of the fourth century it has been observed as the feast of St. Stephen. This distinction was no doubt conferred on him as the first Christian martyr. Of Stephen we know absolutely nothing except what is recorded in two chapters of the New Testament; but there is a " Carol for St. Stephen's Day ", assigned to about the year 1400, which describes him as Herod's Clerk of the Kitchen:

' Stephen out of kitchen came, with boar's head in hand;
  He saw a star was fair and bright over Bethlehem stand.
  He cast down the boar's head, and went into the hall:
  ' I forsake thee, King Herod, and thy workes all;
  There is a Child in Bethlehem born is better than we all.' "

This announcement is confirmed (as in the story of

[1] It is probably a mere coincidence that in some Oriental communities it is commonly said that whoever eats lentils in the twelve days following Christmas will be smitten with the mange.

" The Carnal and the Crane ") by the crowing of a roasted fowl; whereupon Herod commands the tormentors to lead Stephen out of town, and stone him without delay. Apart from the native absurdity of the story, the anachronism would be hard to beat.

The feast of St. Stephen was not very pleasant to horses in days when Dr. Sangrado was a typical medical practitioner. Kirchmeyer tells us that every man drove his horses

> " as swiftly as he can,
> Until they do extremely sweat; and then they let them blood,
> Which being done upon that day they say it does them good,
> And keeps them from all maladies and sickness through the
>   year;
> As if that Stephen any time took charge of horses here."

The custom is said still to survive in Austria and Tyrol. In many parts of Germany, too, and still more in Sweden, customs relating to horses are in vogue—races, cavalcades, feeding the horses with consecrated bread or corn, giving them hallowed salt, and sprinkling them with holy water. It would seem, however, that all this is in honour, not of the Biblical Stephen, but of one Stephen a missionary and martyr in Sweden, who was a great lover of horses, and was slain by the heathen in the ninth century.

The pleasant modern ballad of Good King Wenceslaus and his page " on the feast of Stephen " is said to be founded on traditions of an actual occurrence in Bohemia.

In the north of Yorkshire, till about a hundred years ago, the farmers' wives were accustomed to make large goose pies, which were cut up on St. Stephen's Day and distributed to the poor. One of the pies was usually kept to be eaten at Candlemas. At present, however, outside ecclesiastical circles, St. Stephen's Day is scarcely known in England except by its alternative name of Boxing Day.

But in theatrical circles it has been for several generations *the* great day of the year—the commencement of the pantomime season. In the eighteenth century the theatres were accustomed to present what were regarded as Moral Plays of the type of " George Barnwell " for the edification of the London 'prentices. But toward the end of the century it occurred to the managers that it might be better business to cater for the boys and girls home from school, with a fairy tale or a popular story, leading up to a laughable harlequinade. The experiment proved a complete success, aided as it was by the extraordinary popularity of the celebrated clown Joseph Grimaldi. A generation later managers were accustomed to announce that the new pantomime had been in preparation all the summer. Gradually the proverbial inconstancy of fashion discountenanced the traditional " Harlequin, Columbine, Clown, and Pantaloon ", and demanded sparkling jests, outrageous puns, topical songs, and the like, ending with a gorgeous Transformation Scene. The usual groundwork of these entertainments is still, as of old, a fairy tale like " Cinderella " or " The Sleeping Beauty "; a story from the *Arabian Nights*, like " Aladdin " or " The Forty Thieves "; or a popular folk-tale like " Whittington and his Cat " or *Robinson Crusoe*. Of late years attempts, not wholly unsuccessful, have been made to enforce moral lessons by dramatizing such stories as Dickens's *Christmas Carol* or Kingsley's *Water Babies*, but on the whole the public, especially the children, seem to prefer the non-moral.

St. John's Day, 27th December, is a festival of no great antiquity, having only been established by ecclesiastical authority in the thirteenth century. The only special custom of the day was the drinking, sometimes to excess, of consecrated wine. This was said to be in memory of St. John having drunk a cup of poison from which he received no harm. Some folk-lorists say it was a survival of an old heathen wine sacrifice. All sorts of magical virtues were ascribed to this hallowed wine. Men drank it to make them strong, and maids to make them fair. In Tyrol it was supposed to protect the drinker from being struck by lightning; in Rhineland it guarded the other wine which a man might possess from injury; in Styria it kept the body sound and healthy; in Bavaria it was kept as a medicine against sickness. In Carinthia, Nassau, and other places, some of it was poured into the wine-casks to protect the stock from harm. In the seventeenth century these drinking customs were so rife that scholars maintained with every appearance of seriousness that the German word for Christmas, *Weihnacht*, i.e. " Holy Night ", was merely a misspelling of *Weinnacht*, i.e. " Wine Night ". Probably the truest explanation of the whole was given by a teetotaler, who sagely said, " They drink because they like it ".

The day of the Holy Innocents, 28th December, commonly called " Childermas ", and in Northamptonshire " Dyzemas ", was generally accounted unlucky. It was unlucky to pare one's nails, to put on a new suit, or to begin any kind of work. If any work was begun on that day, it would either never be finished, or would have an unfortunate ending. Not only so: it was held that the corresponding day of the week throughout the next twelve months was likewise unlucky. From the Paston Letters (clxviii, 21st June, 1461) we learn that the coronation of Edward IV, originally fixed for Sunday, 28th June, was on this account deferred to the next day.

In many places it was customary on Innocents' Day to whip the children all round " to make them re-member Herod's cruelty ". In France children who allowed themselves to be caught in bed on that morning came in for a whipping; in Normandy the early risers among the young people themselves gave the sluggards a beating. In the Saxon Erzgebirge the young men whip the women and girls on St. Stephen's Day, if possible, while they are still in bed; and the girls retaliate on St. John's Day. In other parts of Germany the girls on St. Stephen's Day and the boys on St. John's Day beat their parents with fir branches, and the servants beat their masters with rosemary twigs. This is accompanied with a ditty imploring good luck, or long life, for the person who is beaten. That these whipping customs were not restricted to Innocents' Day makes it very unlikely that they were originally commemorative of Herod's massacre. They were more probably—indeed almost certainly—of heathen origin, designed either to expel evil spirits or to confer some magical benefit. They seem related to the Roman

Lupercalia, when young men ran about the streets with thongs, striking every woman they met; the action being regarded as distinctly beneficent. The association of the custom with the Innocents' Day is a mere adaptation.

We have already recorded the custom at Godstow in the thirteenth century, when on Innocents' Day the public prayers were said by children. At a later period there were processions of children on that day, which were suppressed by Henry VIII in 1540. It may be that a notion of literalizing the Scripture precept to "be as little children" suggested a ludicrous practice at Lincoln's Inn in the early part of the sixteenth century; when a "King of Cockneys" was elected, who held a mock court on Innocents' Day. More commendable is a pleasant custom which of late years has been observed in Westminster Abbey, where, on the afternoon of Innocents' Day, a musical service is held specially adapted for children, and Old English carols are sung in procession. This surely deserves to be imitated wherever there are facilities for doing it effectively. In several parishes of West Somerset and Herefordshire it was long customary to ring a muffled peal on Innocents' Day. This practice survived until within living memory.

29th December, before the Reformation, was the ecclesiastical commemoration of St. Thomas of Canterbury, otherwise Archbishop Becket, who was murdered in the cathedral on that day in 1170. References to him are found in several old carols; this, for example:

" The fifth day hallowed St. Thomas,
   Right as a strong pillar of brass
Held up the church, and slain he was,
   And crowned was for his prowess."

But we have not met with any traditional custom on
that day which seems at all related to him, or to the
honour in which he was deservedly held as a champion
of the Church against the usurpations of the civil
power.

30th December, in the ecclesiastical Calendar, is
assigned for the commemoration of two or three all-
but-forgotten saints, of ancient date and purely local
celebrity. The final day of the year is dedicated to
St. Sylvester, Bishop of Rome in the days of Constantine the Great, who figures largely in the monstrous
eighth-century fiction of *The Donation of Constantine.*
No popular custom or tradition is associated with these
" black letter saints ". As to the midnight services
which originated in the early days of the Methodist
Revival, and which are now common far beyond the
bounds of Methodism, they were designed simply as
a solemn consecration of the New Year; and can only
be regarded as an interlude in the Christmas festivities.

In Scotland, before the Reformation, Yule-tide festivities were conducted with so much extravagance and
disorder that the days from Christmas Eve to the New
Year were popularly spoken of as " The Daft Days ".
The violent and revolutionary character of the Scottish
Reformation issued in the abandonment of all ecclesiastical anniversaries; " Pasque and Yule " among the
rest being condemned as relics of Papistry or hea-

thenism. But the proverb holds good, " Though you thrust out nature with a pitch-fork she will return "; and the " Daft Days " were merely transferred to the New Year.

Still, the Puritanic endeavour of the Scottish Reformers to make all things new did not find favour in the Gaelic-speaking districts of the northern Highlands, where customs of pre-Reformation and even pre-Christian antiquity survived till quite recent times. The term Nollaig (cf. Welsh *Nadolig* and Latin *Natalis*) was applied to the whole seven days from Christmas Eve to the New Year. During that time tradition forbade any serious work. The house was decked with holly " to keep away the fairies ", who certainly were not regarded as welcome guests. Christmas Eve was " oidhche nam bannagan ", " night of cakes ", from a custom of giving a cake to every person who entered the house. A slice cut from the Christmas cheese at the feast was supposed to have magical virtues. Familiar sayings were " No Christmas without flesh ", and " Whom Christmas does not make cheerful Easter will leave sad and tearful ".

Other Gaelic customs, relating to the eve of the New Year, seem to be mere survivals of heathenism, and need not be further enlarged on.

49. NEW YEAR'S EVE—HAGMENA

Neither in the Roman nor in the Anglican Church Calendar is there any authoritative recognition of New Year's Day or of its eve. This is owing to the fact that, throughout Western Christendom the ecclesiastical

year was supposed to begin with Advent. But in very
early times every great ecclesiastical festival had its
" octave ", a kind of diminished celebration on the
eighth day; the intermediate days being devoted to
meditation on the topic of the season. Now the Octave
of Christmas, being New Year's Day, came into violent
collision with the heathen festivity of the Kalends of
January, which was often an occasion of much licen-
tiousness. For a time, therefore, the Church in many
places kept the day as a fast by way of protest. But
about the seventh century, if not earlier, it was remembered that, as a son of Abraham, Jesus was " circum-
cised the eighth day ", and received the " Name that
is above every name ". A festival of the Circumcision
therefore supplanted the Octave of Christmas; and,
perhaps by way of compensation, the observances due
to the latter were extended to twelve days. The 1st
of January, however, was not honoured with a vigil
such as had been accorded to most of the greater feasts.

The midnight services with which the New Year
is introduced in some Anglican churches are not, therefore, a survival of ancient custom, but are frankly borrowed from Methodism. In the early days of the
Methodist Revival, about 1741, some colliers at Kings-
wood, who before their spiritual awakening had been
accustomed to spend their Saturday nights in revelling
and drunkenness, began to spend those nights in prayer
and thanksgiving. Wesley approved of their practice,
and commended it, with modifications, to the Methodist Society in London. The devotional meeting was
to be held monthly, on the Friday night nearest to the
full moon. The first such meeting was held on 9th

April, 1742. In course of time the " Watch-night " came to be specialized on New Year's Eve, and, in 1750, Charles Wesley gave to the Church that inspired and inspiring lyric, " Come, let us anew our journey pursue, &c.", wherewith in Methodist circles the New Year is welcomed throughout the world. A custom which long survived in the Lake District, and which perhaps is not yet quite extinct, may be regarded as semi-ecclesiastical; this was to " ring out the old year " with muffled bells, and to follow with a merry peal immediately on the stroke of midnight.

But for the most part the observance of New Year's Eve is ostentatiously secular. There is no need to enlarge on its character as displayed around the Tron Kirk in Edinburgh, in St. Paul's Churchyard, London, and elsewhere when Scotchmen do congregate, " Drinking was and is a great feature of the Scottish New Year's Eve ". Bonfires were lighted in some places " to burn out the old year "; in others a tar-barrel was set on fire and carried about the village, its embers being kept as a charm against witchcraft. Formerly in the Highlands it was usual on New Year's Day to fumigate the house, stables, byres, &c., with juniper, to preserve both man and beast from harm through the coming year. A similar custom persists in Southern Germany, Austria, and Tyrol; the peasant goes with all his household through every room and outhouse, his wife carrying a vessel of holy water, and a censer; every human being, every beast, and even the provisions " must be purified with sacred smoke and the holy sprinkling ". In some places, according to Kirchmeyer, this fumi-

THE WASSAILING OF THE APPLE TREES

From an old wood-cut.

gation was performed on Twelfth Night; and some, he says, repeated it on three nights in succession.

New Year's Eve is a favourite season for divinations. In Germany lead is melted in a spoon over a candle, and thrown into water; omens being drawn from the shapes it assumes. In Lithuania various symbolic objects, usually nine of them, are formed of dough, baked, and laid under nine platters; each person takes up three, and whatever he gets will be symbolic of his future for the year. In Greece two olive leaves, to represent a pair of lovers, are laid on the cinders; as these curl, approach, recoil, or flame up, so will be the issue of the courtship. One cannot fail to observe the close resemblance of these practices to those described by Burns as customary in Scotland on Hallow-e'en, which, as has been said above, was the Celtic New Year's Eve.

An enormous amount of ingenuity has been spent in endeavours to trace the parentage of the cabbalistic word " Hagmena " or " Hogmanay ", which, with its innumerable variants, is found in begging ditties sung on New Year's Eve throughout Western Europe. The classical derivation from the Greek *hagia menē*, i.e. Holy Month, is probably the least likely of all. Not much likelier is a guess that goes back to the heathen Yule-tide, affirming that the night before the solstice was called " Huggunott ", i.e. " Slaughter Night ", with reference either to sacrifice, or to the slaughter of cattle for the feast, or for winter provision: this, with " Mennie ", said to be " the cup of remembrance, always drained at the Yule feast ", furnishes a hybrid and (very improbable) etymology of " Hogmanay ".

Less far-fetched is the guess that derives " Hog-menay, Troleray " from a forgotten French Epiphany carol said to have commenced " L'Homme est né, Trois rois là, &c.". But it seems much more likely that an old French chanty, " Au gui menez, tiri liri, Mainte du blanc et point du bis ", may have been developed, partly by translation and partly by corruption, into the Scottish

> " Hogmenay, Troleray,
> Gie's your white bread and nane o' your grey "

" Gui " is the French name for mistletoe; so that " au gui menez " would be " Lead to the mistletoe ". Miles says this derivation is generally discredited, as well as another from " Au guy l'an neuf ", i.e. " To the mistle-toe the New Year "; but he does not suggest anything more probable. " Aguillanneuf " is used in France both for the last day of the year and for the gift that is then expected. " Aguilando " and " Aguinaldo " are Spanish forms for a Christmas box; " Hoguinané " was Norman French; other forms were " Hoguinano ", and " Ho-guignettes " for gifts. In Brittany the cry was " Au guyané ", and the boys called themselves the " hogui-liannew ". In the Isle of Man a ditty of a similar character was sung by Mummers on the eve of All Saints' Day, which, as we have seen, was the Celtic New Year's Eve—the commencement of winter. It began " To-night is New Year's Night, Hogunnaa ". A very similar form occurs at Roxburgh, and elsewhere in the south of Scotland, viz. " Hunganay ".

Quite a different, it may be an independent, derivation is suggested by the ditty sung at Richmond, in Yorkshire:

" To-night it is the New Year's Night, to-morrow is the day,
  And we are come for our rights, for our 'ray,
  As we were used to do in Old King Harry's day:
  Sing, fellows, sing Hagman-heigh!"

A hagg is an old Yorkshire word for a wood or coppice, and a hagman was a woodcutter. It seems not unlikely that this last version, originating at a time when " Old King Harry " was still in living memory, and wood was commonly used for fuel, may have been the woodcutter's appeal to his customers for a seasonable remembrance.

Another chanty runs thus:

" Rise up, gudewife, and shake your feathers,
  And do not think that we are beggars:
  We are bairns come out to play,
  So come and gie 's our hogmanay."

An old guisards' rhyme recorded in the *Gentleman's Magazine*, 1790, carries a grim suggestion:

" Rise up, gudewife, and be na swe'er
  To deal your bread as long 's you 're here:
  The time will come when you 'll be dead,
  And neither want for meal nor bread."

The same superstitions, now chiefly remembered by way of jest, respecting " First Footings " on Christmas mornings, apply to the earliest moments of the New Year. Many country folk still observe the old custom of opening all the doors in the house a minute or two before midnight on 31st December, and leaving them open until the clocks have struck the hour. This

is called " Letting the old year out and the new year
in "; or, as others affirm, " the expulsion of the Old
Adam and welcoming the New ". In the west of England it was customary, before breakfast on New Year's
Morning, to open the Bible at random, to read the
verse on which the finger happened to rest, and from
it to deduce omens or prognostications for the opening
year.

In several places, both in England, Wales, and Scotland, the first who at midnight on New Year's Eve can
draw from the well a pitcher of " new water " will have
the best luck. (One thinks, perforce, of " the Well of
St. Keyne ".) The water, drunk on New Year's Morning, is a charm against witchcraft and the Evil Eye.
In some parts of Italy the well is decorated on New
Year's Eve; in the morning the girls go as usual for
water, but the lads are on guard, and only sell the water
for nuts, fruit, or kisses.

The first Monday in the New Year is, in various
places, called " Hansel Monday "; the word meaning
" first sale, or use ". It is deemed lucky to receive
money early in the day, and very unlucky to let anything go out of the house before breakfast.

50. OLD CHRISTMAS EVE:
WASSAILING TREES

We have already treated of the Wassail Bowl, and the
ceremonial visit paid to the cattle by the wassailers in
Gloucestershire and Herefordshire; remarking that wassailing in Somerset, Devon, and some other places is

an altogether different, though no doubt related, practice. It is in fact the survival of a pleasant rustic custom, which Herrick thus describes:

> " Wassail the trees, that they may bear
> You many a plum and many a pear;
> For more or less of fruit they bring
> As you do give them wassailing."

The ceremony is deemed proper to old Christmas Eve, i.e. the eve of Epiphany, which corresponds to Christmas, old style. First, a verse of the traditional Wassail Song, " Wassail, wassail, all over the town ", or one of its many variants, is sung: then the company proceed to the orchard, bearing a large jar or bowl of cider. They surround the largest or most fruitful tree, toast it in cider, and dip a branch of the tree in the liquor, or pour or sprinkle cider upon it. Sometimes guns—loaded with powder only—are fired, and kettles beaten to make a great noise. Sometimes three shouts were given, each followed by a blast of a horn; and before each shout all stooped and rose as if lifting heavy sacks. Another custom was to place a crumb of bread or cake and a little salt in the fork of the tree. This appears like " sympathetic magic ". Dr. Rendel Harris thinks it a survival from some forgotten cult of an Apple-god, the apple being perhaps the first fruit in England to be improved by cultivation. The songs—or nonsense verses—that are sung vary in different places; this, from Somerset, seems about the least idiotic:

> " Wassail, wassail, all round the town;
> The zider-cup 's white and the zider 's brown;
> Our zider is made vrom good apple trees,
> And now my vine vellows we 'll drink if you please.

> We 'll drink your health with all our heart,
> We 'll drink to 'ee all bevore we part.
> Here 's one, and here 's two, and here 's dree bevore we go:
> We are dree jolly boys all in a row."

Here is another Somerset chanty:

> " Apple tree, apple tree, I wassail thee
> > To blow and to bear
> > Hat-vulls, cap-vulls, dree bushel bag-vulls,
> > And my pockets vull too, hip, hip, hurrah!"

In Devon and Cornwall the tree spirit was incarnate in a small bird, presumably a robin or tom-tit. He (or it) was represented by a little boy, who climbed the tree, and cried out " Tit, tit, more to eat ", on which a piece of bread and cheese or some cake and cider was given him. The usual ditty was:

> " Here 's to thee, old apple tree,
> > Whence to bud and whence to blow,
> > And whence to bear us apples enow:
> > Barn-fulls, bag-fulls, sack-fulls,
> > Lap-fulls, hat-fulls, cap-fulls:
> > > Hurrah, hurrah, hurrah!"

Of this there were several variants. Either roasted apples or toast was put in the cider jug; and what was not drunk was sprinkled on the trees. The ritual varied in different places. In Devon a pailful of cider, into which roasted apples had been broken, was set in the middle of the orchard; from this pail each person filled an earthen cup, and, going to a tree, drank part of the contents, and threw the remainder, with fragments of apple, at the foot of the tree. A piece of cake dipped in cider was placed in a fork of the tree " for the robins ".

This custom survived in two or three orchards near Minehead (West Somerset) till the early years of the present century. The proper time for wassailing trees was old Twelfth Night, corresponding to 17th January, new style.

In Hampshire, in the neighbourhood of the New Forest, the ditty was:

> " Apples and pears, and right good corn,
>   Come in plenty to every one;
>   Eat and drink good cakes and ale;
>   Give earth to drink and she will not fail."

In Kent and Sussex a kind of half-belief in the value of these incantations appears to have survived almost until within living memory. The Kentish chanty was:

> " Stand fast, root, bear well, top;
>   God send us a *yowling* [1] crop,
>   Every twig, apple big;
>   Every bough apples enow;
>   Hats full, caps full, bushel bushel sacks full,
>   And my pockets full too!   Hooray!"

If no gratuity were forthcoming, this benediction might be neutralized by a curse on the trees. In Kent the rite was sometimes performed in Rogation Week, and in Sussex on New Year's Eve.

51. EPIPHANY

From very early times the religious observances of Christmas were extended to twelve days. Collier (*Ecclesiastical History*) accounts for this by a supposed " law of King Alfred ", to whom tradition has ascribed,

[1] Sometimes " howling " sometimes " yuling ", the meaning of which is doubtful.

with equal probability, almost every old English custom, civil or ecclesiastical. However, the season's festivities usually ended with Twelfth Night, or the Feast of the Epiphany; which since 1800 coincided with the Christmas of the old style or Unreformed Calendar, and was therefore observed for two or three generations as " Old Christmas Day ". Indeed in West Somerset there are traces of " Old Christmas " down to quite recent times. It was especially the horses' holiday, for they were released from all labour, and—according to the kindly precept of St. Francis—received an extra supply of provender. All work on the farm was forbidden; to violate that rule was sure to bring ill luck. But it is uncertain whether this is in honour of Christmas Day, old style, or of the Feast of the Epiphany.

The ceremonies proper to this day were in commemoration of the wise men from the East who were led by the Star to Bethlehem. Patristic and mediæval legend uniformly represents these as kings, and finds in their pilgrimage and offerings a literal fulfilment of predictions in *Psalm* lxxii, 10, and *Isaiah* lx, 6. Their royalty was firmly established in popular belief by the early part of the fourth century. They were alleged to have been baptized by St. Thomas the Apostle; and what were supposed to be their embalmed bodies were brought to Constantinople by the Empress Helena. They were removed thence to Milan; and subsequently, about 1170, to Cologne, where their bones still remain in a costly shrine, the skulls being adorned with jewelled crowns of great value.[1]

The belief that these visitors were kings is respon-

---

[1] See further legends respecting them in section 16.

sible for the curious ceremonial still practised in the
Chapel Royal, St. James'; wherein the king, now by
proxy but formerly in person, makes a formal presentation of gold, frankincense, and myrrh. Down to the
middle of the eighteenth century, the king went in
state, preceded by heralds, pursuivants, and the knights
of the Garter, Thistle, and Bath, in the collars of their
respective orders. But on the insanity of George III
all this was discontinued; and in these days two gentlemen from the Lord Chamberlain's office take gold,
frankincense, and myrrh from a box adorned at the
top with a spangled star, and place them on an alms-
dish held by the officiating clergyman. The ceremony
is very ancient; but we have not been able to trace its
origin. A similar custom existed in Spain. In France
the day is called " Le jour des rois ", i.e. the day of
the kings; and it was so offensive to the Revolutionary
powers in 1792 that its observance was strictly forbidden. Indeed any priest found celebrating it would
have been in imminent danger of death.

In France and Italy, during the Middle Ages, there
were semi-dramatic representations of the Epiphany
not unlike the early ecclesiastical Nativity Plays. One
of them is described in Fosbroke's *Antiquities*. " Three
priests, clothed as kings, with their servants carrying
offerings, met from different directions before the altar.
The middle one, who came from the East, pointed with
his staff towards a star. After mutual salutations and
a short dialogue, a procession was formed, and as soon
as it entered the nave a star resembling a cross was
lighted up, and pointed out to the kings with, ' Behold

the Star in the East!' Two priests, standing on each side of the altar, said, ' We are they whom ye seek;' and, drawing a curtain, showed a child, whom, falling down, they worshipped. Then the servants presented the offerings of gold, frankincense, and myrrh. The mage-kings continued praying till they fell asleep; when a boy clothed in an alb, to represent an angel, addressed them with, ' All things which the prophets said are fulfilled.' " At Soissons the star was represented by an iron circle bearing seven tapers, let down by a rope from the roof of the church.

A more elaborate mummery was exhibited by the preaching friars at Milan in 1336. The three kings appeared crowned, each on a great horse richly caparisoned, and attended by pages, bodyguards, and a great retinue. A golden star was exhibited as going before them. At the pillars of St. Lawrence they met King Herod with his scribes and wise men; they asked him where Christ should be born; and the scribes, having consulted their books, answered, " At Bethlehem ". Thereupon the three kings, having in their hands golden cups filled with frankincense, myrrh, and gold, marched with all their attendants to the Church of St. Eustorgius; the golden star went before them, and they were preceded by trumpets and horns, also by asses, apes, and other animals. In the church, on one side of the altar, was a manger with ox and ass, and the Christ-Child in the arms of His Mother; to whom the mage-kings offered their gifts.

In Italy the gifts, which English, French, and German children expect at Christmas, are often delayed till

Epiphany, when they are supposed to commemorate the gifts of the wise men to the Holy Child. The festival is often personified, like our " Father Christmas "; and the children ascribe the gifts to " Befana ". But Befana is somewhat of a bogie; mothers tell naughty children that " Befana will eat them ".

In Spain the gifts at Epiphany are brought by " the Three Holy Kings ", who go every year to Bethlehem to visit the Holy Child, and leave sweets and toys for good children, who put their shoes outside the window to receive them. In Spain, and also in Provence, the children formerly went out on Epiphany Eve to see the kings pass by. Of course they did not see them; " the kings had passed behind the mountain ". But the children were not long disappointed; after supper they went to church, and there were the kings kneeling in adoration before the Christmas crib.

In many parts of France, Germany, and Switzerland on the eve of Epiphany, boys, and sometimes also girls, went about in masks and strange disguises, shouting, knocking at every door, and making a great noise to scare away ghosts and devils. In other places a mummery was performed, in which the leader carried on a pole a lantern in the form of a star, or perhaps a large gilt star, while the rest sang a carol in its praise. Our Anglo-Saxon forefathers identified the Star of Bethlehem with a certain bright star which they called " Earendel ". In an Anglo-Saxon poem of the ninth or tenth century we find this line, " Hail, Earendel, brightest of Angels ". In some Eastern communities it is said that at Epiphany dough rises without being leavened; but leaven made from this dough must on

no account be lent to any one. At Epiphany the trees
on the banks of Jordan bow and adore the Saviour. Of
wassailing trees on the eve of Epiphany we have treated
already.

52. TWELFTH NIGHT

According to Ecclesiastical Order the evening service shortly after sunset on 5th January is the " First
Vespers " of Epiphany. But in spite of Church Calen-
dars most people will persist in beginning the day with
the morning; and so Twelfth Night commences at
sunset on 6th January.

In Gloucestershire and Herefordshire it was usual
at that time to light twelve small fires and one large
one in a field sown with wheat. This was vulgarly
regarded as a charm to protect the wheat from Smut.
But in Ireland there was a variant of the custom; a
sieve full of oats was set up as high as was conveniently
practicable; twelve lighted candles were set in the
grain, with a larger one in the middle. The original
meaning of these customs is quite forgotten; some say
the fires or lights were intended to symbolize Christ
and His twelve apostles as the Lights of the World,
while others regard them as a survival from the Yule-
fires of heathen Sun-worship.

At Brough, in Westmoreland, there was a custom
which, though observed on Twelfth Night, seems reminiscent of some antiquated form of the Christmas tree.
A holly bush, or sometimes a young ash tree, was prepared by fastening a torch to every branch. These were
lighted; the tree was carried round the village accompanied with music and torches, and was saluted at

certain stations. When the torches had burnt out, the tree was scrambled for by the respective partisans of the two village inns; and the victorious party carried it to their favoured hostel, where the night was spent in merrymaking. In many village inns in the west of England the host "kept open house" on Twelfth Night; the ashen faggot blazed upon the hearth, and

" The mirth and fun grew fast and furious ";

and it is to be feared the virtue of sobriety was not always duly cultivated.

But the Twelfth Night supper was the culmination of all. In the middle of the table was set a huge cake, in which was hidden a coin or a bean, and a pea. The cake being divided, he who had the coin or the bean was saluted as king, and the holder of the pea as queen. (Presumably if a lady drew the bean she would nominate the king, and vice versa.) A mock court was constituted, the offices and titles being assigned by lot; and the fun consisted in the characters being maintained throughout the evening. These characters were written or printed on slips of paper, and drawn from a hat; at least that was the English custom in the time of Charles II. Later, pictorial characters with verses were introduced, which were supplied by pastry-cooks and confectioners. These are said to have been devised by one John Britton, topographer and antiquary (1771–1857). They were at first courtly, historical, or legendary, or taken from the popular comedies of the day. The custom continued till far into the nineteenth century, but was at length killed by the introduction of coarse and offensive characters, like Sir Gregory

Goose or Sir Tunbelly Clumsy. It is not unlikely that the grotesque head-dresses of modern Christmas crackers have some relation to the extinct Twelfth Night characters.

As to the cake, an early recipe informs us that it was made of flour, honey, ginger, and pepper; but in Herrick's time it was an ordinary plum cake. By the end of the eighteenth century it was elaborately adorned with more or less artistic figures in sugar or plaster, often gaudily coloured. We read of one cake in the form of a fortress, with sentinels and flags. Some of the devices were grotesque or humorous. The writer remembers seeing in his childhood, about 1851 or 1852, a cake crowned with a realistic presentation of " the mill where they grind old women young ". The cakes were often of great size, the price sometimes amounting to several guineas.

Hone tells us that in his day, the time of the Regency and of George IV, these cakes made a glorious show in every confectioner's shop window; and it was a favourite prank of the London street boys to pin together the coats or gowns of the people who clustered around, or dexterously to nail a coat to the bottom of a window-frame. Of course this was before the advent of the " new police ".

One Baddeley, an actor, who had formerly been a cook, bequeathed in 1795 a sum of money " to provide cake and wine for the performers in the green-room of Drury Lane Theatre on Twelfth Night ". And to the present time, after the lapse of more than a century, the ceremonial " cutting of Baddeley's Cake " is regularly continued.

In France the king or queen was the only distinguished character used. Usually the cake was cut up, and a child, covered with a cloth, named the recipient of each piece. The first piece was for " Le bon Dieu ", and the second for the Blessed Virgin. These were given to some poor persons; and if either of them contained the bean, the king was chosen by lot. All drank the king's health; and whenever he had occasion for liquid refreshment, the whole company shouted " The king drinks!" The customary Twelfth Night tipple was the "lamb's wool" already described (p. 100). To this Kirchmeyer—or his translator, Barnaby Googe —adds that the Twelfth Night king was

" With shouts and cries
Exalted to the heavens up; who, taking chalk in hand,
Doth make a cross on every beam and rafter as they stand;
Great force and power have these against all injuries and harms
Of goblins, devils, bugs, and sprites, of conjuring and charms.
So much this king can do; so much the crosses bring to pass,
Made by some servant maid, or child, or by some foolish ass."

In the west of England, where the Reformed Calendar was slowly and reluctantly accepted, the ceremonies of Epiphany were for several generations deferred till the twelfth day after " Christmas old style "; so that the old Twelfth Night was 17th January, which was deemed the proper time for Wassailing both the cattle and the orchards.

Christmas was supposed to end with Twelfth Night, which in Normandy was marked by bonfires. In Sweden the date is the Octave of Epiphany, 13th January, called St. Knut's Day. King Knut, who died in 1036, forbade all fasting from Christmas to that date. On that day the young people dance round the table, from which all provisions are then removed; and the household, in a kind of mimic fight, pretend to drive away any guests who may remain.

53. FEAST OF FOOLS, OR OF THE ASS

There was one strange custom, the date of which varied in various places, but which wherever it was observed was regarded as the final close of the Christmas festivities. This was " The Feast of Fools ", otherwise called " The Feast of the Ass ".

In French cathedrals and religious houses, where the inferior clergy were numerous, it was customary in the twelfth century for the deacons to have a merry-making on St. Stephen's Day, the priests on St. John's, and the choir boys on Innocents'. Then on the 1st January (Circumcision), 6th January (Epiphany), or 13th January (Octave of Epiphany) the subdeacons and inferior clergy held a regular Saturnalia. At Vespers, at the words " Deposuit potentes de sede " in the Magnificat, the precentor's staff was handed to the clerk who had been chosen as lord of the feast, and thenceforward the whole service was turned into burlesque. Everything was topsy-turvy; dice were cast and black puddings were eaten on the altar; ludicrous songs were sung, some danced in the choir in grotesque dresses, old leather was burned as mock incense; and in some places an ass was led into the church, in whose honour a ridiculous Latin hymn was sung, with " hee-haw " for a refrain.

At Beauvais, on 14th January, a girl with a child

in her arms rode on an ass into the church, to represent the journey of the Holy Child and His Mother into Egypt: the mass was said, in which the Introit, Kyrie, Gloria, and Credo each ended with a bray; and at the close, instead of the usual " Ite, missa est ", the priest brayed three times, the people responding in like manner. It is strange that such a burlesque of sacred rites should have been tolerated, and apparently encouraged, by ecclesiastical dignitaries, who would certainly have persecuted anyone who dared seriously to criticize either the rites or the opinions on which they were grounded. There are traces of this irreverent folly in Germany and Bohemia; and when at length its impropriety was recognized by those in authority, it had become too popular to be easily suppressed. It was prohibited by the Council of Basle in 1435; yet the last trace of it lingered in the Cathedral of Amiens till 1721.

Here is a fairly close translation of the mock hymn of which mention has just been made; the tune is found in several modern hymn-books, under the name of " Corton ".

Orientis partibus

From the regions of the east
Came this strong and handsome beast:
None with Donkey may compare
For the loads that he will bear.
   Hail, Sir Donkey, hail!

Slow indeed his paces are,
If the cudgel be not there
To inflict a hastening thump,
Or the goad to vex his rump.
   Hail, Sir Donkey, hail!

Christmas Lore

By the measure of his ears,
Lord of asses he appears;
Son of sire who bore the yoke—
Truly an illustrious moke.
   Hail, Sir Donkey, hail!

He, on hills of Shechem born,
Reared beneath a bush of thorn,
Crossed old Jordan's hurrying stream,
Trotted on to Bethlehem.
   Hail, Sir Donkey, hail!

Then for coltish antics queer,
Capering kid and bounding deer,
Midian's dromedaries tall—
Bold Jack-Ass would beat them all.
   Hail, Sir Donkey, hail!

Incense from Sabaea's tree,
Myrrh, and gold of Araby,
At the church arrive at length
By the noble ass's strength.
   Hail, Sir Donkey, hail!

While he draws the loaded wain
With a deal of toil and pain,
Hard the provender he gnaws,
Crunching with his mighty jaws.
   Hail, Sir Donkey, hail!

Barley, with its bristly beard,
Wheat. from chaff and refuse cleared;
Prickly thistles all complete
Make for him a dainty treat.
   Hail, Sir Donkey, hail!

Amen, Donkey, say Amen,
With your chawdron full of grain:
Amen, Amen, yet once more,
Slighting all that was before.
Hail, Sir Donkey, hail!

54. PLOUGH MONDAY, ETC.

Nothing so bad as the Feast of Fools was ever tolerated in the Church of England. But rural England seems to have been loth to resume the ordinary round of labour; for, although Christmas ended with Twelfth Night, it was accounted ill manners to do a full day's work on the following day, jocosely called " St. Distaff's Day ". If the men, coming in from work, found the maids spinning, they would set fire to the flax; and the maids would retaliate by drenching the men with water.

The Monday next after Twelfth Night was called " Plough Monday ". The common explanation of the name is that it was usual to commence ploughing on that day; but in view of the fact that but little ploughing is done in January, some other origin seems to be demanded. It appears that in Catholic times the ploughmen were accustomed to keep lights burning before certain images in the churches, to obtain a blessing on their work. These were called " Plough-lights "; and it is said that the men used to go about in procession on this day to collect money for their maintenance. The Plough-lights ceased at the Reformation; but in many places the procession continued with humorous developments (such as morris dancing and the like), the money being expended in social festivity.

In the north of England it was customary, within living memory, for parties of young men, ludicrously bedizened and harnessed together with ropes, to drag a plough—called " the Fool Plough " (probably a corruption of " Yule Plough ")—round the village, with much cracking of whips and blowing of horns. Sometimes this was accompanied by music and morris dancers, and generally by a fool and his feminine counterpart, called " the Bessy ". The fool was often dressed in skins, with a dependent tail; and the Bessy was commonly a boy dressed to represent an old woman.

Plough Monday is now chiefly remembered in connection with some customary services in manorial courts, which are still rendered on that day.

55. CANDLEMAS

According to the Law of Moses, as understood 1900 years ago, every first-born son was to be presented before the Lord, and redeemed by an offering. This was usually done on the fortieth day from the birth of the child; until which time the mother was accounted ceremonially " unclean ". Our Lord, as became Him who was in all things obedient to the law, was duly presented " after the custom of the law "; and old Simeon, who in all likelihood had heard the strange story which the shepherds " made known abroad . . . concerning this Child ", recognized in Him the long-awaited " Consolation of Israel ", the promised " Light to lighten the Gentiles ". It was quite in accord with the pious sentiment of early Christian ages that this recognition should be commemorated by an anniversary, which should terminate the Christmas cycle, as Holy Thursday does that of Easter. If we may accept the authority of Baronius, this anniversary was observed at Jerusalem as early as A.D. 385, and at Rome during the pontificate of Gelasius, 492–496. In the Danubian province it was observed about 500; at Constantinople about 542; in Gaul in 650; and in England it was mentioned by Beda early in the eighth century. By the Greeks it was called *Hypapantè*, i.e. the feast of *Meeting*; in the west it was the feast of the *Presentation*, or of *SS. Simeon and Anna*; or, among the more ritually disposed, the *Purification of the Blessed Virgin*.

But the prophetic words of Simeon suggested another title, the *Feast of Lights*; of which adaptations and variants are found in many languages. In German it is *Lichtmesse*, in Danish *Kendelmess*, in English *Candlemas*, in old French *Candelière*, in modern French *La Chandeleur*, and in Italian *Candelora, Candelara*, or Sta. Maria *Candelaria*.

These names, and the associated customs, remind us that from of old the use of lamps and candles was customary, though not needed for lighting, yet symbolically, or as a token of rejoicing. It was disapproved by Tertullian in the third century, and by Lactantius in the fourth; but in the fifth century it seems to have been specially appropriated to the feast of the Presentation. Several authorities represent it as a Christianized adaptation of the Roman Lupercalia, when torches and candles were carried in honour of Ceres and Proserpine. However this may have been, in the earlier half of the eighth century there was at Rome on Candlemas Day

a procession with candles, in which the Pope and his
deacons wore black vestments; and on that day " Gloria
in Excelsis " was *not* sung. Of this custom we have
found no explanation.

As to the practice of the Middle Ages, it is related
that " on this day the Church blessed her candles for
the whole year, and made a procession with blessed
candles in the hands of the faithful ". The blessing
invoked on the candles was that " in whatsoever place
they shall be lighted or put, the devil may depart, and
tremble, and fly away, with all his ministers, from that
habitation, and not presume any more to disturb it,
&c.". The candles thus blessed, when used in procession, were commonly lighted from one very large one;
which in Spain was kindled with " New Fire ", i.e.
fire newly struck from flint. The candle-ends were
frequently preserved as charms.

The practice at Rome, about the year 1820, is thus
described: The Benediction was given by the Pope in
person, he being attended by the cardinals in robes
of crimson and gold. After the blessing His Holiness
distributed the candles with his own hand to all present;
cardinals, bishops, abbots, priors, canons, &c., down to
the humblest officials of the Church, going up singly
and kneeling to receive them. The candles were then
lighted, and the Pope, seated in his chair, was carried
round the ante-chapel in procession with chanting.
After this the Pope and cardinals retired, resumed their
ordinary dresses, and proceeded with the usual mass.

Candle-bearing on Candlemas Day was discontinued
in the Church of England by Order of Council in 1548:

but the more conservative of the clergy long persisted in marking the day by the use of an exceptionally large number of tapers. A Puritan preacher in 1628 declared that " On Candlemass Day last past Mr. Cozens, in renewing that Popish custom of burning candles to the honour of our lady, busied himself from two of the clock in the afternoon till four in climbing long ladders to stick up wax candles in the cathedral church (of Durham). The number of all the candles burnt that evening was 220, besides 16 torches; sixty of those burning tapers and torches standing upon and near the high altar, as he calls it, where no man came nigh." The " Mr. Cozens " referred to is John Cosins, afterwards Bishop of Durham.

A contributor to the *Gentleman's Magazine* in 1790 narrates that a few years before, being at Ripon on the Sunday before Candlemas, " he observed that the collegiate church was one continued blaze of light all the afternoon, from an immense number of candles ".

Candlemas is one of the Scottish quarter-days, and was marked by some traditional observances, now obsolete, to the origin or significance of which a clue may perhaps be found in the fact that Candlemas Eve coincides with the festival of St. Bride or Bridget, the friend of St. Patrick, and founder of the first nunnery in Ireland. The connection of the Celtic Church in Ireland with that in Scotland—especially the Western Isles—was very intimate, and many Scottish churches were dedicated in the names of Irish saints. In some of the Western Isles the women of each household dressed a sheaf of oats in a woman's apparel, laid it in a large basket with a club beside it, and just before going to bed cried three times " Brüd is come, Brüd is welcome ". If in the morning there should appear among the ashes what might be thought the impression of Brüd's club, this would be the omen of a prosperous year, and vice versa. " Brüd " can scarcely be other that St. Bride.

The usual dwelling of St. Bridget was Kildare; and there, for several hundred years, a perpetual fire was maintained, nominally in her honour, but really—there can be little doubt—as a survival of pre-Christian practice. The notion of a perpetual fire seems related to the custom of rekindling the remains of the Yule Log on Candlemas Eve, i.e. on St. Bride's Day, quenching it at midnight, and reserving it to kindle the log next year. Moreover, in most schools in the south of Scotland it was customary to kindle a " Candlemas Bleeze ", i.e. a bonfire; not infrequently a growing furze bush, if found conveniently near, would be set on fire: and the boys and girls presented to the schoolmaster donations of sixpence or a shilling—more or less according to the ability of the parents or the popularity of the dominie—as a contribution towards the " Candlemas Bleeze ". The boy and girl who brought the most " bleeze " were acclaimed as king and queen of Candlemas. They were crowned, enthroned, and royally saluted; the whole school was regaled with biscuits and whisky-punch, the remainder of the day being spent in games and merrymaking. One need not be a fanatical teetotaler to be of opinion that the best thing about this custom was its discontinuance.

Football matches, parish against parish, or married

against single, were customary in Scotland, and were keenly contested. Several local and domestic customs have also been reported as relating to the day, mostly connected with candles. The weather, too, was deemed to be indicative of that of the ensuing season, mostly by the rule of contraries; one of several Scottish weather-proverbs runs thus:

> " If Can'lemas day be fair and clear
> There 'll be twa winters in the year."

In England, outside purely ecclesiastical circles, Candlemas is now scarcely recognized except as marking the definite end of the festive season, when—as before directed—the last remains of the Christmas decorations should be removed. Then, as Herrick bids us

> " End now the white loaf and the pye,
> And let all sports with Christmas die."

56. EPILOGUE

In these later years we have been crowding into great cities, and our villages have largely gone to decay. How far this has been the inevitable result of causes beyond human control, or how far it has been brought about by social abuses which are capable of being redressed, are questions for statesmen, which need to be considered in the spirit not of the exchange but of the præsepio. The most poetical of our Christmas customs pertain rather to the village than to the city. And this is natural; it was at Bethlehem, not at Jerusalem, or Babylon, or Rome, that the first Christmas carol was sung, the first Christmas gift presented; and surely we may hope that as a result of increasing wisdom, and especially of a more Christian spirit, in our social legislation, a new era of prosperity will ere long dawn on our villages, wherein we may read the good counsel of old Thomas Tusser without a suspicion of mockery:

> " What good to get riches by breaking of sleep,
>   But, having the same, a good household to keep,
>   Not only to bring a good fame to thy door,
>   But also the prayer to win of the poor? . . .

> " At Christmas by labour is little to get
>   Which, wanting, the poorest in danger are set:
>   What season so fitting in all the whole year
>   Thy needy poor neighbours to comfort and cheer?

> " At Christmas be merry, and thankful withal,
>   And feast thy poor neighbours, the great with the small.
>   Get Holly and Ivy to trim up the house,
>   And take thee good brawn for to seethe and to souse:

> " Provide us good cheer, for thou knowst the old guise;
>   Old customs that good be let no man despise.
>   Yea, all the year round to the poor let us give,
>   God's blessing to follow, by which we do live."

There we have the genuine spirit of Christmas; the spirit that Dickens so delightfully embodies in his inimitable story of *A Christmas Carol* that some cynics would have us believe him to have been the inventor of Christmas. We are not sufficiently up to date to accept this view of the matter; but indisputably the magician who conjured up Marley's ghost has given to the spirit of Christmas a literary setting such as none of the old minstrels ever excelled; and just in proportion as this is realized we shall see the shrivelled heart of Scrooge expanding with its genial warmth, the ghost of Marley effectually laid, and Bob Cratchit beginning to feel that he is not left outside the Brotherhood of Humanity. And so we conclude with Tiny Tim's benediction:

" God bless us, Every One ".

APPENDIX

ADDENDA AND CORRIGENDA

Page 11, lines 11 and following.

In May 1923 the reformed calendar was adopted by the Greek and other Eastern Churches, whose celebration of Christmas now, therefore, coincides with that of the Western Church.

Page 65.

The Advent Antiphons altogether number about a dozen, each of which addresses Our Lord by a distinct title, such as "Wisdom", "Orient", "Key of David", &c. No Breviary includes them all; but usually seven are selected for use on the seven days preceding Christmas Eve. A relic of the old usage remains in the Prayer Book Calendar, in which "O Sapientia" is set against December 16.

Page 133.

Snap-dragon can be traced back to the early part of the 18th century. There was a rustic variant of the game popular in the West of England, called Flap-dragon. A lighted candle was set upright in a can of ale or cider, and the problem was to drink the liquor without extinguishing the light.

Page 135.

A domestic variant of Mumming or Masking appears in the *Acted Charade*, which is said to have been imported from France early in the 18th century.

Page 195.

The central features of the Epiphany festival at Palma de Mallorca, in the Balearic Islands, are the universal purchase on the Eve of the Festa of gifts for " The Babe ", and the Procession of the Three Kings on the day itself.   The cavalcade includes not only the municipal guard and the officers of the local cavalry and artillery regiments, but a horseman carrying a symbolic Star; three heralds in crimson with silver morions; and three groups of " Saracens " who carry respectively a casket of gold, a gilded flagon of frankincense, and a sombre coffer for the myrrh, appropriate to the Three Kings.   These, attired in all the exaggerated finery of the old miracle players, from time to time order a distribution of gifts among the crowd.

On reaching the Town-hall the Master of Ceremonies gravely places on the table of the Alcalde a packet of sweets " for the children of his Honour ", and the procession moves on to make similar offerings to other local dignitaries.

INDEX

Abbot of Unreason, 138.
Abelard, 38.
Advent, 65.
— images, 67.
Africa, savage customs in, 96.
Aguillanneuf and "Aguinaldo", 186.
Ale posset, 121.
Alsace, customs in, 147.
Altar-penny, 166–7.
Ambrose, 37.
Angel, Christmas, 170.
— and shepherds, 52.
Antioch, Roman date adopted, 6, and note.
Apostolic Constitutions, The, 6.
Apprentices, 133, 158, 177.
Ara Coeli, 78, 86.
Ashen faggot, 112–3.
Ashes of the Yule log, 113.
Ass, Feast of the, 200.
Asses, immunity of, 30.
Auguries, 28.
Augustus Cæsar, 3, 4.
— — fabled vision of, 87.
Augustine of Canterbury, 12.
Aurelian, Emperor, 8.
Australia, Christmas in, 170.
Austria, customs in, 151, 176, 184.
Awdlay (blind monk), 58.

Babuska, 146.
Bacchus, 14.
Backsheesh, 159.
Balder, 23.
Bambino, 82, 87.
Bavaria, custom in, 178.
Bay, 18.
Bean, king chosen by, 199.

Beauvais, custom at, 200.
Becket, St. Thomas, 180.
Bees, 165.
Befana, 195.
Bellman's verses, 159–60.
Bells, 68 ff.
Ben Jonson, 40, 134.
Bernard, St., 38.
Besançon, 72, note.
Bessy, 204.
Bethlehem, 73, 80.
Bible, divination by the, 188.
Bills of Fare, Christmas, 120, 125.
Birthday of Christ unknown, 2, 3.
— of the sun-god, 7, 9.
Boar's Head, 117–8, 128–30.
— — at Hornchurch, 129.
— — at Oxford, 129.
— — carol, 118, and note.
Bohemia, customs in, 80, 146, 170.
Boniface, St., 150–1.
Bon Jésus, Le, 148.
Book of Sports, 88.
Boxing Day, 158 ff., 175.
Boy bishop, 84–6.
Bride or Bridget, St., 208.
Brising, necklace, 1, 23.
Briton, John, 197.
Brittany, customs in, 57, 72, 106.
Brough, holly bush at, 196.
Brüd, 208.
Brumalia, 7.
Bush Inn, Bristol, 125.
Bustard, 119.
Byana's Sunday, 173.

Cakes, Christmas, 104–5.
— Baddeley's, 198.

215

Cakes, Twelfth-Day, 198.
Calabrian shepherds, 66.
Calendar, reformed, 10, 11.
Candlemas, 204 ff.
— bleeze, 208.
— Eve, 27.
— play, 59, 77.
Candles, blessing of, 206.
— Christmas, 114, 116.
— procession with, 206.
Candlesticks, notable, 114.
Cards, Christmas, 161–2.
— — forbidden, 133.
Carey, Henry, quoted, 158.
Carinthia, customs in, 151, 178.
Carminow, John, 124.
Carnal and Crane, 55.
Carols, defined, 41, and note.
— collected by Hone, 60.
— French, 46–7.
— German, 47.
— Italian, 45.
— Latin, 48.
— legendary, 54.
— macaronic, 48.
— mystical, 57–9.
— numeral, 57.
— old English, 49.
— origin of, 44.
— psalms as, 91.
— revival of, 61.
— satirical, 57.
— Spanish, 47.
— sung at Court, 62.
— — from church tower, 64.
— — in church, 62.
— use of, 61–2.
— Welsh, 63, and note.
Cattle, feasting of, 149–50.
— kneeling at Christmas, 165.
— visiting on Christmas Eve, 166.
— wassailing, 102.
Census, 3, 6.
Ceres and Proserpine, 205.
Chapel Royal, offering in, 192.
Characters, Twelfth Night, 197.
Charm, a forgotten, 172–4.
Chaucer quoted, 41–2.
Cherry Tree carol, 54–5.
Chester Nativity Play, 76.

Childermas, 179.
Children, festival of, 84.
— preaching, 87.
— procession of, 180.
Christ-Child, mystical presence of, 25.
Christ-kind, 147.
Christmas angel, 170.
— bells, 67–70.
— bonfire, 113, 184.
— boxes, 157–8.
— cakes, 105.
— candles, 114–6.
— cards, 161–2.
— carols, 41 ff.
— crackers, 108.
— crib, 78.
— date, when fixed, 6, 7, and note.
— dew, 105.
— early traditions, 5.
— fare, 119.
— fast ordered on, 91.
— feast, 117 ff.
— fire, 109.
— gambols, 133.
— ghosts, 28.
— gifts, 144 ff.
— hymns, ancient, 37 ff.
— — modern, 60 ff.
— in Australia, 170.
— in New Zealand, 69.
— in Shetland, 170 ff.
— king of, 138.
— letting in of, 108.
— literature of, 35, 116.
— log, 108 ff.
— market on, 91.
— masque of, 134.
— music, 35.
— names of, 11, 12.
— observance forbidden, 92.
— Old, 192.
— origin of, 2.
— pantomimes, 177.
— pieces in schools, 162.
— pies, 107, 122–3.
— prince, 138.
— Puritan hostility to, 88–93.
— rural rather than urban, 209.
— sheaf, 149.

Christmas ship, 155.
— sports, 131.
— superstitions, various, 165.
— suppressed in Scotland, 89.
— tales, 32 ff.
— tree, 157 ff.
— — abuse of, 155.
— — first in England, 153.
— — folk-tale of, 151.
— — lighting service, 154–5.
— — municipal, 154.
— twelve days, 27–8, 175.
Christmas Eve, 36.
— — at Rome, 166.
— — Gaelic, 182.
— — in Holland, 66.
— — in Mexico, 82.
— — (Old), 165.
Churches, decking of, 13.
Circumcision, Feast of, 183.
Clement of Alexandria, 5.
Cleobury Mortimer, custom at, 78.
Coal substitute for Yule log, 111.
Conduits garnished, 25–6.
Conjunction of planets, 3, 4.
Constantine, donation of, 181.
Constitutions, The Apostolic, 6.
Corning, 97.
Cornish pies, 123.
Cornwall, customs in, 190.
Coronation deferred, 179.
Cosins, Bishop John, 207.
Cosmas, St., his hymn, 39.
Court masque, 134.
Coventry Nativity Play, 76.
Coxe, A. C., quoted, 19–20.
Cradle (supposed) of our Lord, 72.
Cradle-rocking, 81.
Crib, Christmas, 78.
Cricket, lucky, 168.
Croatia, customs in, 110.
Crondall, custom at, 64.
Curfew not rung at Christmas, 113.
Cypress, 19.

Daft Days, 182.
Dalmatia, customs in, 110.
Dance of Fools, 97, 124.
Dancing, 133.
— in church, 72, and note, 136.

" Dancing Day " carol, 59.
Date of Christ's birth unknown, 3, 4.
Day of week on which Christmas falls, 167.
Decking of houses, &c., 13.
— forbidden in Spain, 14.
— objections to, 13.
— reasons for, 13.
Dedication, Feast of, 9, 114.
Deer, kneeling, 165.
Denmark, customs in, 29, 99, 105, 152.
Derbyshire, custom in, 24.
Devil Doubt, 96.
Devil killed by an idiot, 99.
Devil's Dandy Dogs, 28.
Devil's Knell, 2, 68–9.
Devon, customs in, 95, 190.
Dewsbury, custom at, 68–9.
Dickens quoted, 163, 210.
Dies Natalis Solis, 7.
Distaff's Day (St.), 203.
Divination, 28, 167, 185, 188.
Dolls, Feast of, 7.
Dough rising without leaven, 195.
Drinking customs, 10, 112–3, 178, 208.
Droluns, 132.
Druidical notions, 20–2.
Dyzemas, 179.

Earendel, 195.
Egyptians, 48.
Epilogue, 209.
Epiphany, 6.
— dramatic presentation of, 193–4.
— fires, 196.
Eve, Christmas, 67, 72 ff.
— — fast in Roman Church, 105–6.
— New Year's (Celtic), 28.
Evelyn's *Diary* quoted, 92.
Evergreens, 12 ff.
— time of placing, 25.
— — of removing, 27.
Exeter, custom at, 62.
Faggot, ashen, 112–3.
Family reunions, 163.
Fast on Christmas Day, 91.
— — Eve, 105–6.
Fasts in Advent, 66.

" Father Christmas ", 146.
Feast, Christmas, 117 ff.
— pigs, 159.
Feasts, coincident, 9.
— profusion at, 119–20.
— subsidiary, 175 ff.
" Figgy Pudding ", 122.
Finland, 64, 115, 152.
Fir, 19.
Fire, the Christmas, 108.
Fires on Twelfth Night, 196–7.
First-footing, 167, 187.
Fish locally deemed seasonable, 106.
Flat foot, unlucky, 167.
Folkstone, custom at, 106.
Follet, Le, 30.
Fool-plough, 204.
Fools, Dance of, 97, 104, 124.
— Feast of, 200.
Football, 90, 130.
Fortunatus, Venantius, 38.
France, customs in, 57, 81.
— superstitions in, 29 ff.
Francis, St., 44, 78, 125, 149.
Freyja, 23.
Friars, 44.
Friesland, custom in, 18.
Frumenty, 121.
Fumigations, 184–5.

Gabriel's Hounds, 28.
Gambling at Christmas, 133.
Games, Christmas, 133.
Gay quoted, 26.
Genealogy chanted, 73.
Genethlia, 11.
Gentleman's Magazine, 187, 207.
German carols, 47.
— customs, 45, 52, 88, 100, 102–3, 122, 128.
Ghosts, Christmas, 28.
— feast for, 29.
Ghost stories, 32.
Giacomo, 45.
Gifts, Christmas, 144 ff.
Gift-books, 160.
Gilbert Davies quoted, 62.
Gipsies, 47–8.
Gladman, John, 140.

Glasgow, punishment for keeping Christmas, 89.
Glastonbury Thorn, 168–9.
Glee parties, 65.
Gloria in excelsis, 65.
Gloucestershire, customs in, 71, 74, 135–6.
Goblins, 16, 28.
Godly ballads, 59, 60.
Godston, custom at, 84.
Golden Age, memorial of, 8.
Golden Bough of Virgil, 20.
Goldsmith, 131, 160.
Gooding, 97.
Goody Twoshoes, 160.
Googe, Barnaby. See Kirchmeyer.
Goose pies, 176.
Great O's, the seven, 65.
Greece, customs and superstitions in, 11, 31, 185.
Greek Christmas hymn, 39.
Gregory I, Pope, 12.
— XIII, Pope, 10.
Grey folk, 172.
Grindal, Archbishop, 136–7.
Guisards, 94.
— rhymes of, 186–7.

Habergaiss, 99.
Hagmena, 185–7.
Hakon, King, 10.
Hallowe'en, 28.
Handbells, 70.
Hansel Monday, 188.
Hans Trapp, 147.
Hanuca, 9.
Haus-Christ, 147.
Heimskringla, 10.
Helga's Night, 172.
Henry VIII, song ascribed to, 17.
Herefordshire, customs in, 71, 135–6.
Herod, death of, 3.
— in Nativity Play, 76.
Herrick quoted, 27, 107–8, 189, 209.
Hickman. See Gladman.
Histriomastix, 90.
Hobby-horse, 95.
Hobgoblins, 29.
Hodening, 97–8.
Hœder, 22, 136.

Hogmanay, 185–7.
Hogs, divination by, 167.
Holland, customs in, 66.
Holly, 14 ff.
— and ivy songs, 14–5.
— bush at Brough, 196.
— He and She, 16.
— in church, 16.
Holy Well (Carol), 56–7.
Home and Household Festival, 1.
Hone, William, quoted, 60–2, 123–5, 198.
Hornchurch, custom at, 129.
Horses, customs relating to, 176.
Hostility of Puritans to Christmas, 88, 90.
Hungary, custom in, 149.
Hunt, Leigh, quoted, 164.
Hunt, The Wild, 28.
Hunting owls, squirrels, &c., 131.
Husk, W. H., quoted, 129, 159.
Hymns, ancient Christmas, 37 ff.
— German, 41.
— Greek, 39.
— Latin, 37.
— modern, 60.
Hymn of the Ass (mock), 201.

Inn, Christmas Bill of Fare, 125.
Inner Temple, Christmas revels, 140.
Innocents, the Holy, 3.
— carol of, 54.
— day deemed unlucky, 178–9.
— — muffled peals rung, 180.
— — observance at Westminster Abbey, 180.
Inns of Court festivities, 139, 141.
Irenæus referred to, 53.
Irish customs and superstitions, 115, 132, 196.
Iron, Trows afraid of, 173.
Italian carols, 45.
— customs, 78–80.
Ivy, 15–7.
— song, 15.

Jacopone, 45.
Janus, Temple (or Gate) of, 4.
Jerusalem, Roman date accepted at, 6, 7, and note.

John's (St.) Day, 178.
Jones, Inigo, 134.
Julebuk, 99.
Julius Cæsar, 10.
Julotte, 63.
Jutland, custom in, 115.
Juvenilia, 8.

Kalendæ Januarii, 8.
Kalendar. See Calendar.
Kallikantzaroi, 31.
Kent, customs in, 97, 191.
Kindel-wiegen, 81.
" King Drinks (The)", 199.
" King of Cockneys ", 180.
King of Christmas, 140.
— mock, 7, 180.
Kings, The Three, 53; legend of, 192.
— — day of their observance forbidden in France, 193.
— — passing by, 195.
Kirchmeyer quoted, 66, 73, 176, 199.
Kissing-bush, 21, 25.
Klapperbock, 99.
Knecht, Rupert, 145.
Knut's Day (13th January), 199.
Kris Kringle, 145.

Lady Bountiful, 117.
Lambswool, 100.
Lampreys, 107.
Lamps in decoration, 13, 114.
Lancashire custom, 115.
Lapland, 63.
Laurel, 18.
Leather unlucky, 168.
Legendary carols, 54.
Lentils, not to be eaten at Christmas, 175, note.
Lights, Feast of, 9, 114.
Lithuania, divination in, 185.
Livonia, superstition in, 31.
Log, 108 ff. See *Yule log*.
Loki, 22.
Longfellow, 75.
Lord of Misrule, 135 ff.
Lord's Day, sanctity of, 88.
Lucy, St., 145–6.
— — as a bogie, 146.

Lucy, St., wife of Father Christmas, 146.
Lupercalia, 180, 205.
Luther, 47.

Mabinogion, 127.
Macaronic Carols, 48.
Madrid, custom at, 72.
" Make Room for Christmas ", 92.
Man, Isle of, customs in, 64, 161.
Manorial courts, 204.
Mari Llwyd, 98.
Market on Christmas Day, 91.
Masking at Court, 134–5.
— pre-Christian, 96.
Mass heard in mines, 169.
— midnight, 71–2.
— probable origin of word, 12.
May Queen suppressed, 141.
Mexico, customs in, 82.
Midnight services at Bethlehem, 73.
— — on New Year's Eve, 183–4.
Milton quoted, 4, 33.
Mince pies, 123, 169.
Miracle plays, 74–8.
Miscellaneous superstitions, 115.
Misrule, Lord of, 136 ff.
Mistletoe, 20 ff.
— Druidical associations, 20.
— kissing under, 21.
— on altar at York, 22, 143.
— on oak, rare, 20, 25.
— song, 23.
— substitute for, 24.
— symbolism of, 22.
Mithras, 9.
Mock king, 7, 180.
" Mock, The ", 108 note.
Moral plays, 177.
Moravian School custom, 78.
Morris dance, 95.
Mumming, 94.
Mumping, 97.
Music, Christmas, 36.
Mystical carols, 57–9.
— reiteration of divine acts, 31–2.

Nadal, 11.
Nadolig, 11.
Nailing up, 198.

Naogeorgus. See *Kirchmeyer*.
Naples, custom at, 66.
Nativity, Feast of the, 11.
— Play at Chester, 76.
— — at Coventry, 76.
— — at Rouen, 73–4.
— — at Wakefield, 75.
— — at York, 75.
— — modern, 78.
Navidad, 12.
Nazianzen, 53.
Necklace Brising, 1, 23.
Neo-Druidism, 98.
Neuwied School, 78.
New fire, 206.
— style, 11.
— water, 188.
— Year, letting in the, 188.
— Year's Eve, 188.
— — Celtic, 28.
— Zealand Christmas, 69.
Newbury, John, 160.
Nicholas, St., 144.
Noël, 11.
— personified, 148.
Noëls, carols so called, 48.
Nollaig, 11.
Normandy, customs in, 76, 138.
Northumberland, Household Book of Duke of, 119.
Norway, customs in, 63, 69, 80, 100, 103, 114.
Norwich pageant, 140.
Nowell, 11.
Numeral Carols, 57.

Oats and candles, Irish custom, 196.
Odin, 28, 98.
— his horse Sleipnor, 98, 149.
Oiel Verry, 64.
Oil of mercy, 153.
Old Oak Chest (story of), 23.
— Style, 11.
Origin of carols, 44.
— of Christmas, 2.
Oracles, belief in, 33.
— silent after Nativity, 33.
Oswestry, custom near, 115.
Owls, &c , hunting of, 131.
Ox and Ass, legend of, 30, 52.

Oxen, immunity of, 30.
Oxen, speaking, 166.
Oxford customs at, 129.

Pantomimes, 177.
Paradise open on Christmas Eve, 169.
Parfre, John, his Candlemas play, 77.
Paris, Christmas trees in, 153.
— customs at, 72.
" Pasque and Yule " abolished, 181.
Paston Letters quoted, 133, 179.
Peacock, 119.
Peckham, Archbishop, 84.
Penshurst, Christmas at, 124–5.
Pies, Christmas, 122.
— monster, 123.
Pifferaria, Calabrian, 66.
Pig customs, various, 127–8.
Pigs, divination by, 167.
Plough-lights, 203.
Plough Monday, 203.
Plum porridge, 121–2.
— pudding, 122.
Plygain, 62–3.
Poland, customs in, 29, 186.
Pomerania, customs in, 148.
Pope blessing candles, 206.
— — sword and hat, 66.
— says three Masses, 71.
Pork, esteemed by Welsh and Irish, 128.
Posada, 82–3.
Præsepio (Presepe), 78 ff.
— curious print of, 83.
Preaching of children, 87.
Presentation, Feast of, 205.
Price, Lawrence, 93.
Profusion in feasts, 119 ff.
Provence, customs in, 109.
Prudentius, 37.
Prynne, William, 90.
Purification, Feast of, 205.
Puritan hostility to Christmas, 88–90.

Queen of May suppressed, 141.
Queen's College, Oxford, 129.

Raging Host, 28.
Rastekais, 29.
Reunions, family, 163.

Richmond, Yorkshire, custom at, 97.
Ringing out the Old Year, 184.
Ripon, customs at, 18, 111, 207.
Ritson, 49.
Robin Goodfellow, 29.
— Hood and Littlejohn, 141.
— Redbreast, 95.
Rome, customs at, 66, 80.
Rosemary, 18.
Rouen, Nativity Play at, 73–4.
Roumania, customs in, 106.
Rumbald's Night, 106.
Ruminant animals kneeling, 165.
Russia, legends told in, 146.
Rutland, superstition in, 25.

Sabbath, Puritan, 88.
— Witches', 96.
Saehrimmer, the Boar, 127.
Saining of children, horses, &c., 172–4.
Salisbury, memorial of boy-bishop of, 85.
" Sally in our Alley ", 158.
Santa Claus, 145 ff.
Saturnalia, 7, 8, 124.
Schimmel, Schimmelreiter, 98.
Schools, Christmas pieces in, 162.
Scotland, customs before the Reformation in, 104, 114, 166, 182.
— Christmas abolished in, 89.
— New Year's Eve and Day in, 184.
Scott, Sir Walter, quoted, 70, 141, note.
Sedulius, 38.
Seeing spirits, 169.
Selden, John, 6.
Serbia, customs in, 11, 110, 126.
Seville, dancing in church, 72, note.
Shakespeare quoted, 32, 100.
Sheaf, Christmas, 149.
Shepherds, Calabrian, 66.
— carol of, 52.
— in Nativity plays, 75.
Shetland, customs in, 170 ff.
Ship, Christmas, 155.
Shoe, receptacle of gifts, 195.
Sicily, customs in, 81.
Sigillaria, 7.
Silesia, custom in, 103.

Sintram, story of, 128.
Sirloin, fable of, 120.
Sir Roger de Coverley, 117, 122.
Sleipnor, Odin's horse, 98, 103.
Snap-dragon, 133.
Solemn League and Covenant, 90.
Somerset, customs in, 95, 188 ff.
Southern Cross, Christmas under, 70.
Sovereign Prince, scripture read by, 66.
Spain, customs in, 72, 193, 195, 206.
— decking with evergreens fobidden, 14.
Spectator quoted, 26, 122.
Spenser quoted, 42.
Sports, Book of, 88.
Sports, Christmas, 130.
Squirrels, hunting, 130.
SS. Simeon and Anne, 205.
Stabat Mater Speciosa, 45.
Staffordshire, custom in, 103.
Standard tree, 151.
— wrecked in storm, 26.
Star-bearer, 66.
Star-man in Poland, 106.
Star of Bethlehem, 2, 3.
Stephen, St., legend of, 132.
— — patron of horses, 176.
Stephen's, St., Day, 175.
Stocking, Christmas, 145.
Stow, John, 25, 135.
Straw, sleeping in, 29, 164.
Strenæ, 8.
Stubbs, J., Puritan, 137.
Styria, customs in, 178.
Sun-god, birthday of, 7, 8.
Sun-wheel, cakes resembling, 173.
Superstitions, various, 165.
Swan, 119.
Sweden, customs in, 29, 99, 105, 127, 146, 153, 176, 199.
Swine, generally disesteemed, 128.
— sacrifices to Frey, 128.
Switzerland, customs in, 86, 146, 195.
Sword dance, 94.
Sylvester, St., 181.

Tales, Christmas, 31.
Tate, Nahum, 60.

Tatler, The, quoted, 36.
Tauler, John, quoted, 156.
Taxing. See *Census*.
Te Deum not sung in Advent, 65.
Telesphorus, Bishop, 55.
" Tenebræ " inverted, 155.
Tertullian referred to, 13, 114.
Thamas-mass, 172.
Thanksgiving Day in New England, 90.
Thomas, St., of Canterbury, 180.
Thomas of Celano, 45.
Thomasing, 97.
Tiberius Cæsar, 3.
Tom-tit, 131, 190.
Tree, Christmas, 150 ff.
— — abuse of, 155.
— — municipal, 154.
— -lighting service, 154.
— of Gold, 151.
— of Life, legend of, 153.
— standard, 151.
Trees, bowing at Christmas, 166.
— — at Epiphany, 195.
— wassailing, 189.
Trolls or Trows, 172.
— — afraid of iron, 173.
— — fond of dancing, 174.
" Truelove to the Dance ", 59.
Tulya's E'en, 172.
Turkey, 119.
Tusser quoted, 210.
Twelfth Day, 196.
— — cakes, 198.
— — Old Style, 174.
— Night, 196.
— — characters, 197.
— — fires, 196.
— — supper, 197.
Twelve days of Christmas, 28, 175.
Twrch Trwyth, hunting of, 127.
Tyrol, customs in, 151, 176, 178, 184.

Unlucky days, 178–9.
" Unthrifty Folk ", 142.

Valkyries, 28.
Vampires, 31.
Venantius Fortunatus, 38.
Visiting the Holy Family, 80–1.

Waits, 36.
Wakefield Plays, 75–6.
Wales, customs in, 62, 106, 127, 130.
Walpurgis-Nacht, 96.
Wassail bowl, 99.
— songs, 102–4.
Wassailing, 90 ff.
— cattle, 102.
— fruit trees, 189.
Watch-night, 36, 183–4.
Webster quoted, 131.
Weihnacht, 12.
Wein-nacht, 12.
Wenceslas, King, 176.
Werewolves, 29, 31, 169.
Wessel-cup, 103.
Westminster Abbey, 180.
Westminster Hall feast, 120.
Whipcol, 173.
Whipping customs, 179.
Whitstable, custom at, 106.
Wild Hunt, The, 28.
Winifred of Crediton, 150.
Wisdom, Book of, quoted, 71.
Wise Men from the East, 3, 53.
Witches and Warlocks, 29.
— — active in Advent, 66.

Witches' Sabbath, 96.
Wither, George, quoted, 40, 158.
Withy carol, 56.
Wood spirits, 13, 25.
Woodward, Hezekiah, 92.
Wren, hunting the, 131.
Wren-boys, 132.

Yew, 19.
Yggdrassil, The Ash, 112.
York, invitation to "Unthrifty Folk", 142.
— dancing in church at, 72, note.
— mistletoe on the altar at, 22, 143.
— Nativity Play, 75.
Yorkshire, customs in, 95, 137, 176.
Yule Baby, 67, 103.
— dow, 105.
— firth, 142.
— -Klapp, 148.
— log, 108 ff; customs and superstitions relating to, 108–11.
— — ashes of, 113.
— — coal as substitute for, 111.
" Yule ! ", shouting, 137.
— straw, 164, note.
Yule, " Yules ", 10, 12, note.